REBELLIOUSLY HAPPY 3-IN-1 COLLECTION

REDISCOVER YOUR SPARKLE, CRAPPY TO HAPPY, EMBRACE YOUR AWESOMENESS

JULIE SCHOOLER

Copyright © 2021 Julie Schooler, BoomerMax Ltd

ISBN: 978-0-473-56336-3

All rights reserved. No part of this publication may be reproduced, distributed, or transmitted in any form or by any means, including photocopying, recording, or other electronic or mechanical methods, without the prior written permission of the publisher, except in the case of brief quotations embodied in reviews and certain other non-commercial uses permitted by copyright law.

DISCLAIMER

This book is designed to give readers some useful tips and ideas. It does not replace expert advice from medical or behavioral specialists. It is recommended that you seek advice from qualified professionals if you are concerned in any way.

This Rebelliously Happy 3-in-1 Collection is dedicated to Marjorie, Tricia and Chrissy

CONTENTS

Reader Gift: The Happy20	ix
REDISCOVER YOUR SPARKLE	1
CRAPPY TO HAPPY	91
EMBRACE YOUR AWESOMENESS	191
Reader Gift: The Happy20	313
About the Author	315
Books by Julie Schooler	317
Acknowledgments	319
Please Leave a Review	321
Book References	323

READER GIFT: THE HAPPY20

Part of becoming rebelliously happy is remembering to squeeze the best out every single day. To remind you of this, I created

The Happy20
20 Free Ways to Boost Happiness in 20 Seconds or Less

A PDF gift for you with quick ideas to improve mood and add a little sparkle to your day.

Head to **JulieSchooler.com/gift** and grab your copy today.

— A *NOURISH YOUR SOUL* BOOK —

REDISCOVER YOUR SPARKLE

REVIVE THE REAL YOU AND BE REBELLIOUSLY HAPPY EVERY DAY

JULIE SCHOOLER

REDISCOVER YOUR SPARKLE

Revive the Real You and Be Rebelliously Happy Every Day

-A *Nourish Your Soul* Book-

Julie Schooler

1
SPARKLE

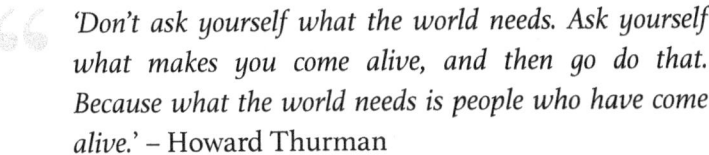'Don't ask yourself what the world needs. Ask yourself what makes you come alive, and then go do that. Because what the world needs is people who have come alive.' – Howard Thurman

No Sparkle

- Do you feel rushed, overwhelmed, tired or stressed out?
- Have you got a fairly decent life... and still feel something is missing?
- When you look back, do you wonder where all that energy and enthusiasm went?

Where did our sparkle go?

What happened to all that fun, love and energy that was overflowing when we were young? What happened to our abundant creativity, our wonder, our innate sense of curiosity, our massive imagination and our ability to easily dream about the impossible?

Our day-to-day living now seems so serious. We are busy being busy. We are switched on all the time. We have so much to do. As a result, we feel stressed, overwhelmed and tired. Oh so tired. Yes, we have responsibilities – work to do, kids to feed, a mortgage to pay, but is this all there is to life?

We look forward to those few minutes of swiping, a sneaky sip of pinot or a long-awaited annual vacation because that is the only time we let ourselves actually have fun and properly rest.

Just because nearly everyone has lost their sparkle and it seems 'normal' doesn't make it right. You still crave it. Deep down when it is really quiet, if you let yourself, you can hear the whispers that tell you that life doesn't have to be this way.

The trouble is, how do you even start to rediscover your sparkle?

Sparkle Recipe

This short book has all the ingredients you need to create a delicious and simple recipe for rediscovering your sparkle. It is brimming with wisdom from top personal development gurus, positive psychology researchers and intuitive ways of living from happy souls who naturally embrace these concepts every single day.

Rediscover Your Sparkle shows how a few simple tweaks to your physiology, mindset and language have the power to take your daily life from tired, stressed and overwhelmed to being full of fun, love and energy.

This guide also cuts through the confusion around meditation, provides compelling reasons why a gratitude practice is a game changer and explains why being extraordinary is your birthright, something you are meant to be.

In a couple of hours this book gives you dozens of no- or low-cost, simple and practical tips to rediscover your sparkle. In doing so, you will revive the real you – the joyful soul that you know is in there but has been suppressed by the seriousness that you have taken on just to get through each day.

You may not believe it now, but you will move from just coping to thriving. Instead of standing on the sidelines of life, you will be dancing in the ballroom.

THE BOOK I WANTED TO READ

I am a wife, a mama of two young kids and a lifelong learner of self-help and personal development. And I am sick of feeling stressed, tired and rushed every single day! There must be a better way to live. Just because everyone seems to feel the same way doesn't make it okay.

So I distilled an avalanche of advice into 'sparkle strategies' designed specially to help busy people just like you and me to uncover our inner sparkle and remember how to love our lives once again.

More than any other book I have published to date, I truly have written the book that I wanted to read. This book is for me. I hope by putting it out in the world that it helps a few of you tired souls as well.

BENEFITS

Just think how great it will be when you rediscover your sparkle. There are so many benefits. You will:

- Bounce out of bed each morning with a zest for life
- Feel like you are in touch with your core self once again
- Gain tools to use language in a more powerful and positive manner
- Uncover how breathing the right way can change your life (yes, really!)
- Improve relationships with those around you from your positive interactions
- Take away some gratitude practice ideas, suitable for morning, noon and night
- Create happiness in day-to-day life without changing a single thing on the outside
- Reclaim all that fun, love and energy you know, deep down, you have inside of you

Sparkle is for Everyone

Busy people are happy to recommend this one short, easy-to-read guide. Readers are relieved that they can finally admit that they have lost their sparkle and want it to return. They are excited that there are profound yet simple ways to be the person they want to be without changing their entire life.

My promise is that if you use even a couple of the suggested strategies in this book, you will feel better, life will be fun again, and you will give the world the best gift of all—someone full of sparkle.

When you rediscover your sparkle, you become a lighthouse for those around you. You won't have to say anything directly. They will notice that your interactions are warmer. They will see that you laugh more readily and heartily. They will want to know the secret to your newfound calmness and happiness.

WARNING: FUN, LOVE AND ENERGY INSIDE!

Don't let that busy and rushed feeling, that negative emotional state and that underlying crappy mood continue to be the norm. It is a cruel and unnecessary way to live. Do not wait another restless night to read this book.

Be the happy person you want to be—not when the 'time is right', but today.

Read this book and you will immediately start to feel more light, energized and playful.

Think of this book as a low-cost luxury, a simple way to rediscover that sparkle you once had. And know that with this tiny luxury comes a bonus: the wisdom in these pages will help you be aware of how meaningful and exciting life can be, right now and for the rest of your life.

2
RECIPE

 'Knowledge is learning something every day. Wisdom is letting go of something every day.' – Zen Proverb

DANDELIONS

My three-year-old daughter, Eloise, let go of my hand. I kept walking a few paces. *What now?* I thought, irritated at the sudden stop. I had heard the bell ring and we were not even close to the school gate to pick up my six-year-old, Dylan. I had planned to be on time but a phone call took longer than I expected, I couldn't find a car park and then Eloise made a fuss about putting her shoes on. A typical day, late to school. Again.

I didn't turn around. "Come on, Eloise!" No response. She was still fascinated with whatever had attracted her attention. She eventually bounded over to me in a few steps. "Look!" She was so excited. It was a dandelion clock: the spherical seed head of dandelion that you can blow on so the white, fluffy 'parachutes' float away. She took a big breath and blew. Simple delight was evident in her face as she watched the dandelion seeds glide away.

I sighed. Looked at my watch. "Come on!" I repeated, even more sharply.

She took my hand and dropped the dandelion stalk on the ground as she marched with me silently through the school gates.

Who is this Book For?

I have written this book for me.

If you get something out of it, fantastic. But I needed to write it so I can remind myself on a daily basis that life truly is awesome.

Too many times I find myself full of anger, resentment and frustration about little things which is then followed up with shame, guilt and despondency as I know I have an extremely fortunate life and I shouldn't be feeling this way.

After all, I live in a relatively safe and abundant country, enjoy good health and am blessed with loving friends and family. I do try to be positive but if tiredness, overwhelm or stress are there – and when are they not? – my response is often less than stellar.

How can I not stop for a few seconds and share the simple pleasure of blowing on a dandelion clock with my beautiful daughter? I have lost the ability to delight in the simple things that my children find so easy to do.

I wrote this book for me, so I don't want to waste your precious time if it's not for you.

Who is this book not for?

- Someone who is truly happy and content with their life
- Negative or pessimistic people who are not prepared to change

Read this book if—like me—you:

- Feel like you are lost in the day-to-day
- Can't just settle for a mundane life on autopilot
- Have a repetitive, persistent thought of 'is this it?'
- Know there must be more to life than how you are living it
- Don't know who you are any more (or perhaps never knew)
- Want to NOT feel tired, overwhelmed, stressed out and stuck
- Have a hunger inside of you, a longing for more meaning in your life
- Want to reconnect with the core you that whispers to you now and then
- Are up for a challenge and willing to experiment a little with your life to bring back that sparkle you know you once had

Please note that if you are going through a diagnosed medical issue, chronic sickness, a life upheaval or a tragedy, there are more suitable books and resources out there to support you, although the tips in here can help as well. And if you suspect your issues may be coming from a more serious cause—perhaps an undiagnosed mental or physical illness—I don't want to diminish the seriousness of your situation. Please seek appropriate professional advice.

Still here? Great!

Let's get this party started.

What is 'Sparkle'?

There is no dictionary definition for sparkle in the context that it's discussed in this book. There are some great synonyms - vivacity, animation, liveliness, vitality, exuberance, verve, high spirits, zest, effervescence, enthusiasm, vigor, spiritedness, dynamism and fire - but nothing truly captures sparkle.

It's easier to describe its opposite. It's obviously not the stress, tiredness, overwhelm, frustration and irritability I seem to have in spades.

It seems nebulous, but, like a sturdy umbrella in a downpour, you know when you have sparkle and when you don't. My daughter has an abundance of sparkle. I do not.

My definition of sparkle is anything that highlights or emphasizes fun, love and energy.

Rediscovering your sparkle means remembering how to have fun in a way that is right for your life. It involves finding out what you love the most and doing more of it. Sparkle also helps to revive your energy with activities that light you up.

Bringing more fun, love and energy into our lives is a critical thing to do yet we dismiss it, turn away from it or ignore it. We have the best excuses for not accepting more sparkle in our life but do they really stack up? More on that in the next chapter. For now, let's assemble a recipe for sparkle.

S-P-A-R-K-L-E Ingredients

Rediscover Your Sparkle

The letters in the word 'sparkle' are a perfect framework to rediscover your sparkle. The seven 'ingredients' in the 'S-P-A-R-K-L-E' acronym will help you tap into ways to love your life on a more consistent basis.

Each ingredient has three suggested strategies to bring about more fun, love and energy into your daily life. These are explained further in the next few chapters, but here is an outline:

Savor

Play

Appreciation

Rest

Kindness

Lightheartedness

Extraordinary

RECIPE FOR SPARKLE

Here is the recipe to help you rediscover your sparkle:

- Mix together savor, play, appreciation, rest, kindness and lightheartedness
- Add a generous dollop of fun, love and energy through suggested strategies
- Bake in some acknowledgement of just how extraordinary you really are
- To create a delicious life you absolutely love

You don't need to be a Michelin-star chef to cook this. It's an incredibly simple recipe yet it's not easy. None of these ingredients of sparkle may seem fresh to you but are you deliberately nourishing yourself with them in your daily life?

The title of this book starts with 'Rediscover' rather than 'Find' for a reason. Isn't it great to know that the recipe for sparkle is simple wisdom that you can reintegrate back into your life?

I could have made this book much longer but I wanted to get to the good stuff! I agree that we need to change our negative thoughts, regulate our emotions, revise our bad habits and address the limiting stories we tell ourselves. In my book *Crappy to Happy*, I delve into these areas.

But as author and podcaster, Gretchen Rubin says, "The absence of feeling bad is not enough to feel happy–you must strive to find sources of feeling good." Please, by all means, investigate these matters but why not adopt a few of the sparkle elements into your life as well? Why wait?

Let's tap into what makes us sparkle right now.

Let's build ourselves up, give ourselves the utmost indulgence and care and then address the mindset shifts that help us to improve our lives even more. Yes, we need to work on ourselves but why not try this as a starting point? A focus on rediscovering our sparkle will make our life brighter and is very likely to lead to some of our negative behaviors effortlessly falling away.

But... I Want More!

We had sparkle as children, but as time wore on, we grew up, became more serious and were heaped with a bunch of responsibilities. Our sparkle faded away.

The elements discussed in this book are sufficient to bring back your sparkle but they are also only the first rung or two on the ladder to a richer life. Attributes such as curiosity, wonder, courage, empathy, dreaming big, believing in the impossible, creativity, easily cultivating friendships, intuition, imagination, not worrying what others think and pure joy were in abundance in my childhood but now they have almost vanished.

First, we need to go back to basics before we try and access these loftier concepts. Savoring leads to wonder and curiosity. It is hard to use your creativity when you haven't let yourself play. And it is almost impossible to access your intuition unless you give yourself space to rest. You won't dream big if you don't embrace the extraordinary human you are.

Sure, we all have some of these traits left but they are not nearly as plentiful as they once were. I am creative enough to write a book but it's been a long while since I have completed 15 artworks with complete joy and abandon each and every day like my daughter does at kindergarten. And I set goals but have lost some of the imagination and dreaming big that my son has, like, for instance, when he tells me all the gifts he wants for his birthday.

It's easy to think these traits are a childhood indulgence, not appropriate for adults to focus on. But deep down we know that these intangible qualities are what makes life worth living.

Concentrate on the simple sparkle suggestions first and watch as they unlock all the other 'childlike' attributes that we long for. The recipe for sparkle is a gateway to our grander ambitions.

All Aboard!

The next chapter will go over the objections raised against rediscovering sparkle. These may seem reasonable, however they are... well, they are just garbage. The following six chapters will discuss the main ingredients of sparkle, which lead to the final chapter and seventh element – living an extraordinary life.

In each chapter, a variety of suggested strategies will be presented to help you revive your sparkle. These will relieve pressure and boost you up so you can face the day. The sparkle strategies are meant to help you and not stress you out! If you feel overwhelmed, note that they are merely suggestions. Choose what seems most delicious to you and try it out. Many are not about adding stuff but about eliminating something nasty from your life.

I am not going to advise you to *Eat Pray Love* around the world. These are mostly low-cost suggestions to help you enjoy your life as it is right now. You really can be happier without changing your life in a drastic way.

The chapters end with three challenges that reflect the suggestions to improve your sparkle. Implement ones that resonate the most with you for a day or a week. Then, if you wish, add them into your life in a way that feels right. Assess how you feel afterwards and if you don't feel even a little more sparkle, go back to how you were.

Sparkle Movement

Rediscovering our inner sparkle means getting right back to the basics, finding ourselves and appreciating what we truly love once again. This is so critical that I want to generate a sparkle movement. Through my book, *Super Sexy Goal Setting*, I am seeking a goal-setting revolution, so why not a sparkle movement as well?

I would love a whole bunch of people to deliberately take action that invokes their sparkle each day.

Can you imagine a world where even a tiny percent of us did that? Even 1% more sparkle in the world – wouldn't that be better? How much lighter it would it feel? How much more fun, love and energy would be cascading around us?

I want to create a sparkle movement.

I hope that you will join me.

3
OBJECTIONS

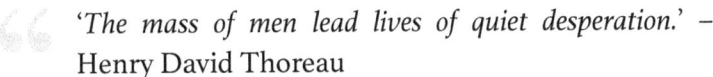 *'The mass of men lead lives of quiet desperation.'* – Henry David Thoreau

Novels

I read not one, but two disappointing novels over the festive break. This is not the most tragic thing in the world, but it stung more than I thought it would. Why was I so bitter about reading a couple of mildly unsatisfying books?

The main reason was that I had heaped way too much anticipation onto the two novels. They were unlikely to have ever stood up to my gold-standard expectations after months and months of almost solidly reading non-fiction.

Don't get me wrong; I do enjoy non-fiction, very much. But I love novels too and I had tipped the scales far too much in one direction. In the past few years, I very rarely let myself 'indulge' in reading fiction even though it makes me really happy.

Why would I not do something that I absolutely relish?

Rollercoaster

We can all agree, at least in theory, that rediscovering your sparkle is a good thing for ourselves, our loved ones and humanity, yet there is a lot of resistance to it. I understand this. Boy I do! I have raised every single one of these objections in its various forms.

This chapter will be a rollercoaster but by the end of it you will be able to glide seamlessly into the best ways to rediscover your sparkle.

Strap yourself in.

Objection 1 – Self-Indulgent

Reading novels, especially since I had kids, seemed like an indulgence, a frivolous and almost selfish waste of time. In other words, I decided that reading for fun was not that important to me. After all, I'm a grown up and novels were just another childhood luxury I must relinquish.

One of regrets from the book, *The Top Five Regrets of the Dying* is "I wish I had let myself be happier." Yes, it may seem strange but we CAN choose to be happy. Every single day.

The very fortunate get to attain some happiness in their work, but if this is not the case then we can notice what makes us happy and lean into that. It may not be reading novels, but you will have something you currently think of as an indulgence, something you think of as a bit frivolous, maybe even selfish.

Do that thing.

Do it today.

And if you don't know it yet, there are plenty of opportunities to figure it out during the rest of this book.

OBJECTION 2 – TOO BUSY

You may not come right out and say that you are too busy to be happy, but this objection can be expressed in other ways. You may say that you don't have spare time or that your family or work is your priority right now or that you are too exhausted to contemplate yet another thing you should do at the moment.

Somehow, I led myself to believe that I was too busy to do one of the handful of things I absolutely love to do most in the entire world – reading novels.

And yes, of course, like you, I lead a big, full life, but I often slide into prioritizing things that do not contribute to any real, lasting happiness. Instead of reading a book I can find myself watching a banal sitcom, shooting off an email so I can keep my inbox down and scrolling, scrolling, scrolling. Sometimes all at the same time.

Maybe I cannot lose myself in a novel on a rainy Sunday afternoon for hours at a time like I did when I was younger. But I can still go to bed a half hour earlier or read a book on my phone in five-minute increments while waiting in line.

We all have the same 24 hours in a day, and someone out there is swimming under a waterfall, learning how to juggle or strumming their favorite song on an acoustic guitar and you are not. Are you busy being busy without adding value into your life? Our culture celebrates busyness! Don't confuse this with living a fulfilling life.

Please stop lying to yourself that you are too busy - or too tired from being so busy - to bring a bit of sparkle back into your life.

Objection 3 – Not Built for It

Some people say they can't rediscover their sparkle as they are simply not that happy and never have been. Here is the truth – being happier is harder than not being happy. Let that sink in for a moment.

Every single human on the planet has a negativity bias. Due to our need for survival in prehistoric times we had to be on alert for anything that may harm or kill us. We are on constant alert for attack or lack. Our conditioning means that we are more likely to notice the negative than the positive. This is our default position, so we have to train our minds to notice and accept the joy that is prevalent in the world.

There is this pervasive cultural belief that happy people are just the lucky ones, born with genes that allow them to be happier, always able to look on the bright side. They naturally have a sunnier disposition without having to work on it. And yes, there is some science around a 'happiness set-point' and some people do find it a bit easier to be happy, but that does not mean that it's not achievable for the rest of us. There is still plenty of leeway for us all to tap into more happiness.

First, however, you have to stop lying to yourself that you are just not built for it. Not being supremely happy is not our fault – our minds are not designed that way – but it is our responsibility. And now you know that, you can't go back.

Objection 4 – Don't Know How

The objection that you don't know how to be happy is a little sneaky as it will let you believe that you want to rediscover your sparkle but you don't know how to attain it so it's probably not worth pursuing.

Would you say that you really want that vacation but don't want to call the travel agent or learn how to book the flights yourself so you won't go? Would you say that going on vacation is too hard? You can poke holes in this 'don't know how' excuse very quickly.

Happiness is not something that happens to us; a lot of the time we have to cultivate it. Being happier is hard work but that is what makes it worthwhile.

Okay, can we now all agree that doing things that make us happy is important, that you could find room in your busy life for some more sparkle and that even though you are not built to be happy you are willing and able to find out how to create more fun, love and energy in your life?

Let's get more candid and admit that what is stopping us is not the tactics or the how-to but our mindset. On the surface, it may seem strange to have fears attached to something that seems so desirable, but it's perfectly natural. After all, now we have to admit that something is missing from our lives and we want it back.

OBJECTION 5 – FEAR OF STANDING OUT

Any time we strive for more, for something we really want, there is fear attached. One way this shows up is a fear of attack. For instance, we don't want to stand out, be different or make a fool out of ourselves in our quest for more sparkle. We want to be 'normal' but keeping to society's standards means a mediocre existence as we default to negative thinking unless we work at it. You wouldn't be reading this book if you were content with that.

Yes, rediscovering your sparkle means showing up, embracing your weird self and being enthusiastic about life, even if others judge you. I constantly have to remind myself that I would rather remain uncool yet exuberant than part of the downbeat in-crowd any day of the week.

Objection 6 – Fear of Not Deserving It

Our fears stem from our prehistoric minds. Attack – if I show my sparkle, people may judge me. Lack – in pursuing sparkle I may lose something else.

I have a recurring negative thought pattern that tells me that I don't really deserve the peak level of happiness that reading a novel can bring me.

There is a bug in my system that constantly reminds me that since others have such real tragedy and horror in their lives, and my life is fairly fortunate, then who am I to strive for soul-filling joy? I tell myself that I have 'enough' and so shouldn't want for more.

However, as Bronnie Ware explains in *The Five Regrets of the Dying*, we don't have to feel guilty about happiness – "it is a lighter feeling that we all desire."

A few weeks ago, I entered an online competition to win a pile of novels – and, just like that, I won it. This could be just plain luck, but I would like to believe it was the universe telling me that not only was it acceptable, but absolutely essential to read more fiction this year. When nine novels literally land on your doorstep, it does make you reassess what you thought was true.

Rediscovering your sparkle is about desiring, not about deserving.

OBJECTION 7 – FEAR OF EMOTION

We can now admit we want sparkle back in our lives. We desire it, we crave it, we need it. But here is the main roadblock: rediscovering your sparkle will get you to *feel* once again.

Going on this journey means getting back in touch with our positive emotions. This is hard because anyone who seems truly happy can be considered at best, naïve and at worst, certifiable. How can anyone be happy when the world is on fire?

Even more challenging: by allowing in the positive emotions, we also have to feel the so-called negative emotions – you can't feel just one type of emotion. And once you let yourself feel, you will feel everything. Everything.

You will feel sad that you didn't do this sooner, angry that you missed out on the delight and wonder of life for so long and scared, so very scared, that once you regain your sparkle you could lose it again. It's something you have denied yourself of for so long and now you don't want to let it go.

We are so used to numbing and distracting ourselves these days that acute emotions – of any type – are avoided at all costs. After all, no one likes to cry during a performance review or get the giggles at a committee meeting. Being in touch with your emotions puts us in a vulnerable state and this can be incredibly uncomfortable.

I understand this. The world breaks my heart. I care about too many things. How can I strive to live with sparkle when there is child slavery / domestic violence / plastic filling the oceans / corrupt politicians / tigers disappearing off the planet? It's all too much. What do I focus on? What is more important? How can I help when I can barely get through the day? I can't even pick up my child from school on time so tackling climate change seems a little out of my league.

As I write this book, a horrible tragedy has occurred here – 51 lives lost in a senseless and horrific mass shooting that has shaken my tiny country and the whole world. How can it even be possible to write a book about rediscovering your sparkle when there is so much hate in one person that it would cause him to carry out such an atrocious act? How can I think anything I do makes a difference?

I simply want to rediscover my sparkle so if my daughter shows me a dandelion clock again, I will stop and appreciate it. But maybe, just maybe, if that person had reconnected with his core self and found something he could focus his love on, this massacre wouldn't have happened.

Rediscovering your sparkle doesn't mean that you will suddenly deny all the horror and hurt in the world. It means tapping into all of your emotions – both 'good' and 'bad'. It is boldly seeing all the trauma and suffering yet not letting it suck you in and consume you as well.

Pursuing your sparkle means deliberately and bravely trying to be happy.

Admit that you are making excuses that are stopping you from rediscovering your sparkle. And then move forward. Please, please, please, do things that make your heart sing, things that light you up. Do them even if you still believe these objections. Do them because you read a book today that told you to.

. . .

Your Comfort Zone

People think they don't want to leave their comfort zones, as they feel nice and familiar, and they feel safe and in control of their environments. Going to work, coming back to your home, watching TV, these are all nice at times. Being in your comfort zone is comfortable, but after a while it actually starts to hurt you. You start to feel unenthused and jaded with your routine existence.

The real magic happens outside of the comfort zone. If the magic happens outside, why do you want to stay inside? Your negative and misleading thoughts tell you that it's impossible to live the life of your dreams.

Let's get this straight right now: you are responsible for your life; you create your life. Not the latest political scandal, not your current family drama, not a nuclear threat. You. If you are just going through the motions in life controlled by fear, then it is up to you to find a way to change. Don't let the story you tell yourself stop you from being truly happy and fulfilled.

The challenges that are coming up in the next chapters will deliberately try and get you out of your comfort zone of crappiness and launch into an uplifting place. For the first baby step however, you don't need to leap for euphoric joy. Instead, practice stepping out of your comfort zone with some neutral tasks. This will help train your brain to not default to its usual, mostly negative patterns.

Challenges

Try these for a day or extend them out to a week so you can feel, and move through, some of the difficult emotions associated with stepping out of your comfort zone.

Challenge 1 – Replace the current ring tone for your mobile phone

Challenge 2 – Set the radio station onto one you never normally listen to

Challenge 3 – Put on a different top, socks or watch - something you rarely wear

4
SAVOR

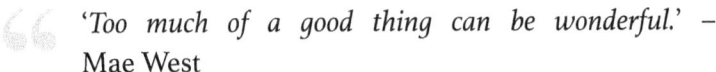 *'Too much of a good thing can be wonderful.'* –
Mae West

SNAILS

Becoming a mama has changed the whole course of my life and has been the most challenging yet magnificent thing I have ever done. I have learned a lot about myself, being a parent and balancing (juggling?) everything. I expected there to be a steep learning curve in all these areas.

What I didn't anticipate is how having kids has helped me find out what is truly important in life. My children remind me on a daily basis to live life to the fullest. I may be the one imparting knowledge but they divulge the real wisdom.

A few months back, when I picked up Dylan from school, he ran off with his friends to look at a snail. Yes, a snail. When I joined him, after finishing a conversation, more than five minutes later, he was still poking around that poor snail, trying to cover it with a leaf and feed it some crumbs. Eloise was marveling at the creature as well.

As adults, we don't do this. We don't savor. We almost never 'stop and smell the roses', and so miss out on the awe and delight that savoring can invoke. Children remind us that the world around us is full of wonder and I, for one, want to make sure I remember that.

Mindfulness versus Savoring

Oh, you say, you are talking about mindfulness. We are told to be mindful all the time. We just did a mindfulness seminar at work. I know I should practice mindfulness more often. But you know how it is. Busy and all that.

Yes, I do know how it is! We are 'shoulding' all over ourselves! I don't want you to feel like you 'should' do this. I want you WANT to do this.

This is mindfulness but with a sparkly twist.

Please hear me out.

Mindfulness is a trendy concept these days, but it simply means bringing your attention to the present moment. It has exceptional benefits: it is linked to improved focus, better performance at work, more positive emotions, increased self-knowledge, higher self-control and greater empathy amongst many other things. This sounds great but to rediscover your sparkle I think we can go one better.

Savor means 'to delight in / enjoy' (Merriam-Webster Dictionary). It is not just about noticing but extracting enjoyment from the moment or activity for as long as you can. Savoring, or its associated words, luxuriating, reveling, marveling, relishing or basking are simple methods of finding pleasure in everyday moments.

Doesn't savoring sound a lot more exciting than being mindful? Mindfulness is hugely important, of course it is. It's just that savoring, well, it's more fun. It may be a slight language variation, but let's go with it.

We agree that savoring sounds incredible so why don't we savor more? We are constantly distracted by our phones, rushed by our hectic schedules, future focused and want to 'save time'. These are cultural constructs that we don't have to buy into. Saving time, for instance. What does that even mean? What do we 'save' it for? Instead of saving time we need to savor. Savor not save. See what I did there?

Each sparkle element can be incorporated into our lives in a multitude of ways. This book features three suggestions for each. Some help you eliminate the excess that blocks our sparkle. Others help us to gracefully allow sparkle back into our lives.

The challenges at the end of each chapter will invite you to incorporate these suggested strategies into your life. They should feel like a welcome addition, something you didn't realize you were craving all along, that easily slots into your routine.

You can read these chapters in any order and take actions on any of the suggestions as you wish but I advise to simply follow the path laid out for you. After all, if you have not taken delight in a snail in the past few decades then you need to start at the beginning.

SAVOR STRATEGIES

1. Eliminate Distractions
2. Take Two
3. Savor Long Time

STRATEGY 1 – ELIMINATE DISTRACTIONS

With advertising blasting at us from every corner, video so easy to record and watch and the prevalence and pervasiveness of social media, we are more distracted than ever before. Did you know that we typically spend over three hours per day on our smart phones? Or that, on average, a phone is picked up an incredible 50 times per day? Or that – and this is embarrassing – 70% of us look at another device while watching TV?

It was hard enough a few years back to stay focused, but now, as Jen Sincero says in *You are a Badass*, we are so distracted it is a wonder we still speak in full sentences. This may seem obvious but in order to start savoring our real life, we must reduce our – mostly digital – distractions.

Ways to do this:

1. Turn off your push notifications. PLEASE people! You don't need the latest celebrity tweet or WhatsApp group message flickering onto your smart phone screen every four seconds. Keep your important calendar reminders on but turn the rest of them off! I am not going to tell you exactly how to do it as it is different for each device. Start by going into your settings for the relevant apps and switch any push notifications to OFF. Please. Now.

2. Do a digital declutter. Don't know where to start? Here are some ideas: unsubscribe from emails you don't need (especially those daily deal ones), delete emails that you have read and taken action on, remove apps you don't use and unfollow social media

pages, groups and people that you don't want to see in your feed any more.

3. Change your habits with your smart phone or device. Things I try to do:

- No second screen in the room while watching a TV program or movie.
- Only look at social media three times per day – once in the morning, once around lunch and once in the evening.
- Not give my phone a quick glance any time I am waiting or could be bored, like when I am standing in line, waiting for the kids to finish something or, er, at the traffic lights. If it's a short wait I challenge myself to look around. Yes, at the world. Notice things. If it's a long wait, I always have an interesting article saved or a book to read on my Kindle or Apple Books apps on my phone.
- Bonus tip: wear a watch. When I wear a watch I am not pulling my phone out to look at the time and then swiping to check something.

Yes, these are difficult at first but I didn't say finding your sparkle would be easy. I said it would be worthwhile.

Strategy 2 – Take Two

Due to our prehistoric survival instincts, humans build neural pathways more effectively in response to negative experiences than good ones. To help our minds, we need to take a few more seconds to install the positive bits. We need to savor, marvel and bask, to slow down so our brains have time to take in the pleasure and override our natural bias to the negative.

Now we have removed (or extensively minimized) some of our major distractions, let's uncover a way to savor that is short and sweet. This suggestion costs nothing, only takes a few minutes and allows us to delight in our everyday world.

Take a two-minute break three times per day and do any of the following suggestions:

- Cloud, star or moon gazing
- Shake it all out and do a quick stretch
- Close your eyes and notice smells around you (works well in a café)
- Look up from your screen and gaze out at the view (this is good for your eyes too)
- Step outside, feel the sun on your skin and listen for the sounds of what is around you (birds, insects, traffic, talking, etc)

You get the picture. Do something that taps into your physical senses, resets you and keeps you present. It will make you feel refreshed, less alone and usually very blessed. Link 'Take Two' to another daily habit such as waiting for your morning coffee or add three alarms or calendar reminders into each day to help you to stop and savor.

An optional component of 'Take Two' is to allow yourself to sound out your savoring. Say "mmmmmm" or "wow" or whatever comes naturally to you. Sounding out savoring is a great indicator that you are basking in the moment.

Strategy 3 – Savor Long Time

Start with 'Take Two' and then if you are game, move onto longer activities. Here are two suggestions:

Listen to a whole album from start to finish. I am not talking about a playlist or a greatest hits compilation but one set of songs from one artist or band. Download something, pull out an old CD or dust off your vinyl collection. Put the album on when you are doing something physical like tinkering in a workshop, cooking, gardening or doing housework. Allow yourself to be swept away by the music. Dance to it if the moment takes you there.

Have a long, leisurely dinner and really take in the textures, smells and tastes of the meal. Actually chew 30 times each mouthful like your grandmother told you to do. Out at a restaurant is preferable for this, especially a very nice one that does all those little courses, but any time you eat and fully appreciate each taste is a bonus. I know this is all but impossible with young kids but maybe serve them earlier and then try it for one dinner without them sometime.

Make Delight a Habit

Savoring may seem like an instant gratification idea but it takes practice and dedication to make it a habit so it's a permanent part of rediscovering your sparkle. It is not skimming across a screen to whatever is the next shiny object but paying attention and delighting in the world around us.

Removing our screen obsession is important to begin to savor once again but it's even more critical when it comes to the next ingredient in the sparkle recipe – play.

Challenges

Challenge 1 – Do a digital declutter in any way that benefits you the most, e.g.: remove push notifications, have an email unsubscribe-fest and delete apps that you don't use

Challenge 2 – Each day: 'Take Two'. Take two minutes, three times each day to savor

Challenge 3 – Once this week: listen to a whole album from start to finish

5
PLAY

 'Life must be lived as play.' – Plato

WATERSLIDES

A few months back, I took my six-year-old and his friend to some pop-up waterslides, set up on a temporary basis while school was out over the summertime. The boys were booked in for a two-hour session so I traipsed up the hill with them at the start and made sure they were safe and having fun. Then I retreated to the shady parents' area.

I hadn't even contemplated going with them but after a little while, I stopped being able to concentrate on my book as a little voice deep inside me kept insisting I go on the waterslides. Like, right now.

There wasn't a single good reason to stop myself so I raced to get changed into my swimsuit and headed for the waterslides. I went down at least 10 times! It was honestly the most fun I had in a very long time. It was so awesome that I was charged up, not just for the rest of the day, but for quite a while after. I truly believe that the one hour spent on the waterslides helped me get through the rest of the school holidays with a smile on my face.

And this, my friends, is the profound power of play.

NOT JUST FOR KIDS

Play is the second essential element of sparkle and yet it is so easily neglected. The thought of play can actually stress people out as it means things – important, serious things – are not getting done! We all can agree we've enjoyed playing in the past but now we are grown up it seems like a waste of time.

Even though researchers such as Dr. Stuart Brown from the National Institute of Play argue that we have a biologically programmed need for play and have listed its benefits from fostering empathy to triggering our creativity, we tell ourselves that playing is not as important as our mile-long to do list.

Charlie Hoehn points out in his fabulous book, *Play it Away* that if you dedicate 30 minutes per day to play, that only adds up to 2% of your week. When I decided to go on the waterslides, without 'too busy' to use as an excuse, I realized what stops me from playing is a bunch of fearful thoughts: that waterslide looks quite big and scary / you will look silly as one of the only adults there / you will freeze at the top of the hill while waiting to go down again / your swimsuit could come down / you could stand on something sharp while walking back up etc. We fear standing out or looking silly or hurting ourselves or not being 'good' at it. And yes, there is a risk of all these things.

But the risks of not playing are far greater: Dr. Stuart Brown argues that the opposite of play is not work but depression.

Let's see how we can incorporate more play into our lives.

Play Strategies

1. Say 'No'
2. Create a 'Playlist'
3. Schedule Play In

Strategy 1 – Say 'No'

This is for the people out there who still say they have no time to play. There is an easy fix: say 'no'.

Prioritizing play will mean some things need to be shed from your life. You need to remove the good to make way for the great. Putting boundaries around your playtime will be difficult, at least at first. If you do not learn to say no, then you are saying 'yes' to someone else's agenda and 'no' to yourself.

You can still be a lovely person and say 'no'. Author, researcher and TED speaker, Brené Brown says "Compassionate people ask for what they need. They say no when they need to, and when they say yes, they mean it. They're compassionate because their boundaries keep them out of resentment."

If you are unsure whether to say no to a future commitment, ask yourself if you would do that very thing tomorrow. Tomorrow is probably already booked up solid so if you still want to do that thing then say yes, otherwise say no. As author and entrepreneur, Derek Sivers, says "If you're not saying HELL YEAH! about something, say NO."

Even in the nicest way possible, saying no is uncomfortable, so practice on small things and build up. Here are a few ways to say no politely:

- "Sounds wonderful, but that is not part of my work focus right now."
- "Sorry but my current commitments mean I cannot take that on."
- "It sounds amazing but I wouldn't be able to give that the attention it deserves."
- "I can't help you right now but I can schedule it after X date."
- "Sorry it is not my policy to do X." (People respect policies, even ones you have made up yourself!)

If a 'no' is done well, people should be happy with how clear you are and how committed you are to what is important to you. And if they are not happy? Well, their response is their problem.

Strategy 2 – Create a 'Playlist'

I believe that all the stories we tell ourselves about how we are too busy to play or that it is a waste of time or only for kids and all the fears we let in about play are a big cover up for the actual problem about playing as a grown-up – we have forgotten how to do it.

> We don't know what we like, what really lights us up, what genuine fun even is any more.

Let's face it, in today's world where we all worship at the altar of busyness and distractedness, when is the last time you had good clean fun? I don't mean finding happiness at the bottom of that glass of pinot or in the latest scroll or swipe, but in real life: the waterslide kind of fun. You need play. You have just forgotten how essential it is.

What play means to you is different to what it means to others. In *Play it Away*, Charlie Hoehn mostly defined play in terms of the traditional 'move outside in the sunshine with some friends' kind. I was stumped by this for a while. I didn't want to play catch! But then I realized that the concept of play can be broader than that.

Play can simply be thought of in terms of what you absolutely love to do: activities that bring you joy and things that are fun for you.

This is an extension of the first sparkle strategy for play: Say 'No'. We are not just making room for play but for the actual play we really want to do.

Think back to when you were a kid plus what you prefer to do as an adult in your extremely limited spare time and make a list of activities that you would like to do more of. Remember too that play can be on your own or with others. Deliberately turn toward something you want to do as opposed to 'should' do or that everyone else seems to find fun.

Writing your 'playlist' may take a while and can be added to over time. It's fine to start with the more traditional things that others enjoy, then you can cross them off later when you tap into what you truly like to do.

Here is my playlist:

- Practice some yoga / sun salutes / stretches
- Listen to and dance to music I love

- Read a great novel or interesting non-fiction book (including audio books)
- Chat with like-minded people about personal development, writing or books
- Go to a film, concert, festival or comedy show
- Walk in nature when it is fine and sunny e.g.: forest or beach
- Eat out at a nice restaurant (once in a while, not all the time)
- Visit a book store and have a good long browse
- Bake yummy treats with my kids
- Short, fun trips away with family or friends
- Fun games like disc golf, mini-golf and casual games of table tennis
- Playing Pacman on an old-fashioned arcade machine
- And of course, waterslides (at times)

You may love to do entirely different things. Here is a bunch of things I wouldn't find all that enjoyable but you may be craving to do: craft activities and scrapbooking, playing a musical instrument, painting or sculpting, hanging out with your favorite pets, team sports or playing catch in the park.

Really get down to the nitty gritty and personalize your 'playlist' just for you.

Strategy 3 – Schedule Play In

You must put play in your calendar or diary.

This goes against the spontaneous and organic nature of play but so what? If we don't schedule in time to do what we love then it won't get done.

Utilize your calendar or diary system in the best way possible. If there is one play activity you want to do this week then block out time for it. If you want to do something every day (go to bed earlier to read a novel, play a board game with the kids etc.), then get a wall calendar and 'don't break the chain'. Put a cross on the calendar for every day you take action and try to keep that chain of crosses going.

Make scheduling play a playful task. More on being playful in a later chapter.

Change Your State

Play is a fantastic ingredient to rediscover your sparkle as it mostly uses your body to actively change your state. The next chapter on appreciation is a great complement to this body focus as it exercises the mind.

Challenges

Challenge 1 – This week: practice saying no, at least once, in the politest way possible

Challenge 2 – Create your 'playlist' - a list of things you would absolutely LOVE to do

Challenge 3 – Schedule in a 1 x 30-minute session for play in the next week. Bonus points if you manage 30 minutes per day of play for a whole week

6
APPRECIATION

 'Gratitude is the wine of the soul. Go on. Get drunk!' —
Rumi

RAISINS

"Raisins."

This is the reply I often get from my almost four-year-old daughter when I ask her what she is grateful for. It has become a bit of an in-joke between us. I have been asking her what she is grateful for since she was two, long before she really understood the concept. Back then she often said "Raisins." I am not exactly sure why. Now she can give a wide variety of great answers but if she is feeling particularly silly or perhaps is a bit stumped, she reverts back to her usual: "Raisins".

When I do my own gratitude exercises, I appreciate that my daughter has a wicked sense of humor!

. . .

Why Don't We Practice Gratitude More?

Cultivating appreciation creates awareness of the good in your life and invites in some more positive thoughts that will start to nudge out some of the many negative ones. Being grateful for the small miracles of daily life—the super computer in your back pocket, the sunshine on your face, your child's laughter—makes you feel like you have enough and that your world is abundant, not lacking.

Gratitude studies have shown that an appreciation practice is associated with being more enthusiastic about life, being interested in the community, being kinder to others and getting better sleep. One study found participants were a whopping 25% happier after only a short time of practicing gratitude.

And yet many of us are not all that appreciative. Like savoring and play, we tell ourselves this is because we are too busy. A ridiculous excuse when saying "thank you" can take less than a second.

Another reason for the absence of gratitude is that we think that we don't know how to do it 'properly'. One way this 'don't know how' excuse can be believed is when there is debate about whether you are practicing gratitude or practicing appreciation and whether there is a difference between the two. It is easier to debate the semantics all day long than to simply say thanks.

Look, there may be some variation between gratitude and appreciation but I use the terms interchangeably. I called it 'gratitude' in my book, *Crappy to Happy*, but here I mostly call it 'appreciation' as otherwise it wouldn't fit in the S-P-A-R-K-L-E acronym! Choose a word that resonates with you and simply decide to be more thankful. Anything else is just a procrastination attempt to stop you from doing something that can quickly return the sparkle back into your life.

The real reason we don't practice appreciation relates to our deeper fears and worries. We think that if we acknowledge how thankful we are for our fortunate life, we will invite disaster. Won't putting emphasis on what we appreciate somehow turn our reasonably happy life upside down?

Like the other parts of rediscovering your sparkle, practicing appreciation is simple but not easy. As Brené Brown says in *The Gifts of Imperfection*, practicing gratitude can be a vulnerable act and we must tolerate some of the discomfort of vulnerability to whole-heartedly soak in gratitude or else it will be accompanied by our scarcity mindsets and fear of loss.

The absolute best way to get over the slight discomfort of scarcity fears attached to appreciation is to practice, practice, practice.

Incorporate gratitude in your daily life at any opportunity.

Here are three suggestions to do just that:

APPRECIATION STRATEGIES

1. Thank Your Bed
2. Practice Gratitude Daily
3. Massive Appreciation Exercise

STRATEGY 1 – THANK YOUR BED

I thank my bed. Yes, I thank my bed. I got this tip from Louise Hay, motivational author and founder of the publisher, Hay House. Thanking my bed is both ridiculous and profound. Ridiculous as I am thanking an inanimate object. I get a little giggle from doing it, which puts me in a great mood. It is also profound as I realize how fortunate I am to be sleeping on a bed each night. I find that most things that are worthy in life are both ridiculous and profound.

Thanking my bed is also a great way to start the day. Like many things in life, particular care should be taken with the start and end of things, with take offs and landings, and thanking your bed is a good way to 'take off'.

Strategy 2 – Practice Gratitude Daily

Endings are important, too. That is why the gratitude practices that are suggested below happen in the evening, although any time of day is good. Find a time of day and a practice that you can stick to and do it every day. It is the everyday nature of appreciation that is important, not what you do, how long it takes or even what your responses are.

Do this exercise on your own or with your partner or kids on the way to school or work, over breakfast or dinner or, especially, at bedtime.

Ask the following two questions:

- What are you grateful for?
- What are you happy about?

I often say something more profound, life affirming or esoteric for my grateful answer (the sun, clean running water, healthy kids, etc.). Then I respond with something more ridiculous or materialistic or frivolous for the happy one (my favorite TV program, chocolate or a new podcast I have discovered). You can list many things or settle on one. This is where Eloise, my daughter, comes up with 'raisins'. The answers are not important, the practice and the redirection of thoughts is.

There are many other appreciation practices you can adopt instead of, or as well as, the one above. I don't recommend taking these all on as that would be too overwhelming! Select one or two that resonate with you and make them into a habit.

- Start a gratitude list and share it via email with a few friends
- Write a list in a journal of three or more things you are grateful for each day
- Put a sheet of paper on the fridge that everyone can add a gratitude item to
- Once a week, at dinnertime, speak your appreciation to others at the table
- Create a 'Gratitude Photo Album' of images you love and keep it private or share it on social media
- If you can't get to sleep, do an alphabet appreciation exercise: think of something you are grateful for starting with A then B etc – believe me, you won't make it to Z

STRATEGY 3 – MASSIVE APPRECIATION EXERCISE

Author and entrepreneur, Tony Robbins has a method to get out of a funk and allow cheer to return after dealing with negative emotions. This brief exercise turns up the volume of positive emotions so you flood yourself with them and end up with a higher emotional baseline. It shifts your state from crappy to happy. You are not replacing the negative with the positive; you are not 'pushing it down'. The negative is gracefully released and now you are inviting the positive back in.

Give yourself three minutes for this activity. First, close your eyes, place your hands onto your heart and breathe deeply and slowly. Feel your heart's strength and power and its miraculous ability to keep you alive and well without you even thinking about it. Then think of three moments from your past (yesterday, five years ago, when you were a child or any time) that make you feel immensely grateful. Fully step into those moments and vividly remember the grace, magic and beauty of those times. Finally, think of one thing you can be joyful about right now. Perhaps your heart beating? The fresh air around you? The beautiful memories you have access to at any moment? Now open your eyes, smile and move on with your day.

Believe me, it is almost impossible to feel bad after soaking yourself in appreciation in this way.

Just Say Thanks

These are wonderful suggestions but you don't have to get all fancy with appreciation. Just try to say 'thank you' more throughout the day. Saying 'thank you' is a polite and easy way to bring appreciation into your life, only takes a second or two and a genuine thank you may make someone else's day.

I sent off a two-sentence email to someone thanking her for a particular podcast episode I found inspiring. When I got in contact with her again, over six months later, she remembered my kind words. She had not only told her friends and family about the email but said it had helped her continue with her podcast.

> **Giving her a quick thank you took me a minute and it made her whole week.**

Savoring, play and appreciation are all exceptional strategies to invoke sparkle but they won't get you anywhere unless you decide to prioritize rest. It may seem dull but, as we will see in the next chapter, rest is a vital component of rediscovering your sparkle.

CHALLENGES

Challenge 1 – Thank your bed every morning straight after you wake up

Challenge 2 – Choose a gratitude practice and stick to it each day for a week

Challenge 3 – Attempt the massive appreciation exercise once this week

7
REST

 'The amount of sleep required by the average person is five minutes more.' – Wilson Mizener

SLEEP

When I was pregnant with my first child, I was given a lot of well-meaning advice for impending motherhood. But when it came to the recommendations about sleep, I disregarded them as I was one of those lucky people who happily thrived on five or six hours per night. I didn't think that having a newborn baby would impact on my sleep that much.

How wrong can one woman be?

There is simply no way to prepare yourself for how little sleep you may get in those first months with a newborn. I developed what I coined 'sleep stress' (try saying that ten times fast). What the books didn't say was how difficult it was to know whether Dylan would have a 15-minute catnap or sleep for three hours.

In those first few weeks, I got to the stage where I would be happy if I managed to lie down and close my eyes in a dark room for ten minutes. I also developed 'sleep jealousy'. I would get a visit from a friend who told me they had a sleep-in or an afternoon nap and I would literally see green. If someone told me that they had had eight hours of sleep in a row, I would almost break down in tears at the thought of such an unheard-of luxury.

During the nastiest times in those first few months with a newborn I actually found myself hallucinating. I thought I had a conversation with my husband but he wasn't even home. I made stupid mistakes like trying to towel-dry myself in the shower cubicle before I turned the water off.

Now that I am way past the newborn stage with both my kids, now that – knock wood – they sleep through the night, I have a much better appreciation of sleep. However, it still never feels like enough.

Why do we not allow ourselves to rest?

Not a Luxury

Rest is the least, well, *sparkly* of all the elements of sparkle but it is an absolute necessity. Without rest we simply cannot function, let alone sparkle. Sleep is not a luxury but we treat it like one. There are many reasons for this – our pursuit of more, the cultural requirement to be busy at all times and the many 'shiny object' alternatives to actual proper rest like the next must-see show that has just dropped.

I believe however that it is deeper than that. I always believe it is deeper than that! Because we have lost the sparkle in our lives, we try to make it up with things that we think will make us happier or give us some short-term pleasure or escapism but are not actually contributing to our sparkle.

We wake in the morning, race around like a lunatic all day long, finally 'get it all done' or most of it done to a point we can be satisfied or can partially ignore the next urgent task until tomorrow, then find out it is already 9.30pm and don't want to go to bed yet because we haven't actually done anything we truly wanted to do! We haven't done anything that would bring some sparkle into our day.

At this point, we are too tired to actually do something active, even something we might love like reading a book. We are certainly way too exhausted to do one of the things we 'should' do, like work on a hobby, meditate or even wash our face properly. So instead, we passively watch whatever is on and by then its after 11pm so we roll into bed, read two pages of that juicy, fat novel and fall into a restless sleep.

Er, is this just me?

If we took time to savor, play and appreciate, even in short intervals during the day, we would allow ourselves to properly rest as we have already given ourselves what we truly crave – the nourishing activities that bring us love, fun and energy.

As inspirational speaker and trainer, Alexander Den Heijer says: "You often feel tired, not because you've done too much, but because you've done too little of what sparks a light in you."

Hopefully you have started building in some of the first elements of sparkle into your life. Then you will actually want to rest properly so you can enjoy your life to the fullest. But if not, please read on and try and incorporate rest as a habit. Doing so will make the sparkle strategies listed in the other chapters even more attractive.

Please note that if you feel chronically tired, then it is worth seeking professional help. You may have an underlying thyroid, hormonal, adrenal or another issue that is not being picked up. At the very least, I suggest you read life coach, Louise Thompson's book: *The Busy Woman's Guide to High Energy Happiness* or nutritional guru, Dr. Libby Weaver's *Exhausted to Energized*.

REST STRATEGIES

1. Breathe
2. Meditate
3. Sleep

STRATEGY 1 – BREATHE

We have 20,000 opportunities each and every day to boost our health and happiness—every single time we breathe.

Most people breathe shallowly, only using the upper parts of their lungs. This type of breathing keeps you in your sympathetic nervous system (SNS) and hence holds you in fight or flight mode.

It's time to relearn how to do slow, deep belly breathing. Yes, relearn—it is how babies naturally breathe. These belly, or diaphragmatic breaths invoke your parasympathetic nervous system (PNS) and hence your rest, digest and repair systems. Your body slows down and starts healing. When the PNS is active, the SNS cannot be dominant, which means it is more difficult to be on alert and stressed.

Breathe in through your nose and count to four so that your stomach gets inflated, like you are filling up a balloon. Hold that breath for a count of four. Then breathe out through your nose or mouth to a count of four and hold it for another count of four. Don't worry about the nose/mouth thing—do whatever comes naturally to you. Also, don't worry about how many seconds you take with the inwards and outwards breaths and holding it. Just make sure your stomach gets inflated, which means that your lungs are filling up with oxygen.

This is meditation teacher and wellness expert, Davidji's '16-Second Meditation'. I know you are busy, but you have 16 seconds to spare, don't you? Do this as much as you can during the day as a mini reboot to the present. It helps to link it to other daily activities like waiting for the tea to brew, showering and at a red light.

If you don't take anything else from this book, promise me that you will relearn how to breathe right. Do your own version of the 16-second meditation every day.

We have already talked about savoring – taking some short breaks during the day to drink in the fine world around you. Taking some deep breaths while you savor is the perfect way to crank up all the goodness that savoring brings.

STRATEGY 2 – MEDITATE

Meditation is an ancient practice dating back thousands of years. It has been around for millennia because it works. Maybe you tried it but felt like the imperative to clear away all your thoughts was too hard. Perhaps you couldn't commit to an hour a day. Possibly you didn't know if you were doing it 'properly'. After a time, you stopped. Now it seems like just another thing on the long to do list that you will never cross off.

You do not have to clear away your thoughts. Your job in meditation is to observe your thoughts and let them go by without judgment. You do not have to commit more time than you can fit in to meditate each day. The benefits of meditation have been shown with a practice that takes as little as three minutes per day. Meditating every day is the most important thing. You can't meditate 'wrong' unless you are checking Facebook or driving or mowing the lawn while you are doing it. For a traditional meditation practice, a quiet space where you are unlikely to be interrupted for a few minutes is the ideal, but even that is negotiable. Your subjective experience of the meditation is not that important. You may feel bored, fidgety and that you have tons of thoughts, but you still may be in a deep meditation without realizing it.

The point of mediation is to give your mind a rest. A constant practice will calm the mind and leave some space. Less chatter means a clearer head, a more focused mind and more energy. The goal of meditation isn't to control your thoughts but to stop letting them control you.

Numerous studies have shown a direct link between a consistent meditation practice (even a few minutes each day) and almost every positive health and wellbeing outcome you can think of. It has a beneficial impact on medical issues like nausea, ulcers, anxiety, even diabetes and heart disease. It has lowered pain intensity and decreased the length of the common cold. It has been shown to boost positive emotions like compassion and reduce negative ones such as loneliness in the elderly and post-traumatic stress in veterans. Meditation actually changes brain function and can help with focus, creativity and maintaining longer periods of productivity. No wonder modern workplaces are embracing it.

If you want to 'get something out' of meditation like it is some sort of transaction, then spend some more time investigating the myriad of benefits it offers. But remember there is no competition when it comes to meditation. Your own practice may improve over time, but the only 'winners' are those who commit to it every day.

Think of meditation as a little daily luxury, a treat, something you can do just for you. Give yourself permission to do nothing for at least three minutes, then try to build up to ten.

Find a meditation practice that you like and will keep doing. This may take some experimenting, and this is fine. First, find a quiet place and a good time each day to meditate. Favorites are in bed before getting up in the morning or last thing at night, in a parked car before work or in the evening straight after dinner.

It doesn't matter whether you sit up or lie down. You don't have to sit in a certain posture or lie in a particular way. You don't have to wear anything special or light candles or anything. Sit or lie so you are comfortable. If you think you may fall asleep, that is fine, especially for a nighttime meditation. If you don't want to fall asleep, then set an alarm to go off at the end of the three (or ten) minutes.

In order to let your thoughts drift through your mind, many meditation practices encourage concentrating on something in the present. One such thing is the breath, so you can concentrate on your breath going in and out. Another way to concentrate on the present is to adopt a mantra. This can be linked to the breath, for example, in breath—peace, out breath—calm. At the start, your thoughts will override this practice almost every second, and all you do is get back on track again and again: 'Oh that is a thought about the laundry, breathe in peace, breathe out calm'.

Alternatively, there are guided meditations you can follow. These can cost money and will require headphones, but may make meditating easier. You can find guided meditations all over the Internet or you can buy CDs, MP3s or download meditation apps such as Headspace.

The best thing about a guided meditation is that you can concentrate on the music or voice and not the chatter in your head. And even if you don't listen to it 100%, even if you feel your mind drift, you will still get a lot of the benefit of meditation from relaxing and breathing deeply. I have found guided meditations the easiest way to commit to a meditation practice each day.

Strategy 3 – Sleep

Look, I am not going to tell you how to sleep, when to sleep or how long you should sleep for. I am not even going to suggest the best nighttime 'get ready for bed' routine, how you shouldn't have screens in your room or where to purchase blackout curtains. Goodness, I am not even going to tell you to go to bed at the same time. I do none of these things myself.

You KNOW you should get more sleep, just like you know you should drink more water, exercise daily and eat a lot of vegetables. We all know to do this stuff; we just don't do it.

Here is what I suggest – go to bed half an hour earlier each night than you usually do. That is all. That is likely to give you over three hours more sleep each week. Doesn't that sound amazing? Three extra hours of beautiful slumber each and every week. That's the equivalent of over 150 hours or almost 20 full nights of sleep in one year!

If you would prefer an actual bedtime then go to bed with lights out by 10pm. Author and speaker, Marci Shimoff calls this "catching the 10 o'clock angel train". Set an alarm on your phone for 9.30pm and when it goes off – start getting ready for bed. My night alarm says 'STOP FAFFING AND BRUSH YOUR TEETH'. Feel free to use the same wording if it's the kick up the proverbial you need to get the rest your body so obviously requires.

Encore

Let's practice belly breathing right now. With me, take a deep breath so your stomach expands out, hold it for a few seconds and then exhale it out. Doesn't that feel good?

Breathing the right way is crucial - yet perhaps a little ordinary method - to rediscover your sparkle. If you want something a bit more spectacular, keep reading as the next chapter kicks sparkle up a notch with its focus on kindness.

Challenges

Challenge 1 – Breathe – do a deep breathing exercise intermittently throughout each day

Challenge 2 – Meditate – do three minutes of meditation every day for a week

Challenge 3 – Go to bed, lights out by 10pm every night for a week

8
KINDNESS

 'No act of kindness, no matter how small, is ever wasted.'
– Aesop

My Not-So Secret Hurt

Just after Dylan turned two, we were delighted to find out that I was pregnant again. That delight turned to despair a few weeks later when I had an early-term miscarriage. Trying to make sense of my emotional reaction, I did what I always do – write. It was a cathartic way to deal with what happened. It was only after I finished that I knew I had to post it on my blog.

At that time, only a few close friends and family members knew that I had been pregnant so posting a blog about my miscarriage for the world to read was risky. But the point of the blog post ended up being a wish to open up the conversation about pregnancy loss and miscarriage so it seemed like the right thing to do.

I had absolutely no expectation as to the impact of that one blog post. I was surprised when many women opened up to me about their own experiences. A lot of people forwarded it to friends and said it helped them. And I was swamped with beautiful comments and kind wishes. One friend even left a box of chocolates with a thoughtful note on my doorstep.

One of the darkest times in my life turned out to be a wonderful way to have honest conversations, permit myself to be vulnerable and allow others to express their compassion and empathy. I didn't ask for kindness but it was ready and waiting when I needed it the most.

Why is that? I believe we have a lot of kindness inside of us that is just looking for an excuse to get out.

Top Tier

We are told that giving to others makes us happier. Of course, we know that kindness is important. We are not monsters! To be happy, we must give our joy out to the universe freely and abundantly. But when we feel rushed, tired and overwhelmed, giving is just another thing that can make us feel, at best, smug, but more often, resentful.

It helps to think of kindness in an alternative way. Give because you know your happiness counts. Give because if you are happy then others around you are more likely to be.

Give because it grants you a richer life.

Remember, you need to feel fulfilled yourself before you give. Fill yourself up with the other sparkle elements first and then attempt this top tier recommendation. Remember to do some deep belly breaths each day, meditate, express gratitude, savor life's pleasures and give time over to activities that you absolutely love and that are fun for you. Only after all that is it a good idea to give to others more than you do already.

Kindness Strategies

1. Listen
2. Wish Happiness
3. Random Acts of Kindness

Strategy 1 – Listen

One simple, free way to give more is to listen to others. Like savoring, listening is a lost art. We have two ears and one mouth but we don't prioritize them in that order.

Practice active listening. Let the other person finish what they want to say, without interrupting or finishing their sentences. Look them in the eye and act interested. Then ask them at least two follow up questions on the topic without relating it back to yourself at all. If you are not sure what to ask, say these three little words: "tell me more."

Sometimes it is hard to listen actively and deliberately create constructive conversations. When we are lacking sparkle, it's all we can do not to slump and scroll. On these occasions, the best way to be kind is to simply not lead with the negative. Don't start with a criticism.

Start with adoration

Now when my kids come out of their rooms with odd socks on or ruffled hair, I try to stop myself from critiquing or tidying them up and instead, pause, smile and remind myself what teacher and author Toni Morrison says: "Let your face speak what is in your heart."

After all, kindness always starts with a smile.

STRATEGY 2 – WISH HAPPINESS

Something you can do that takes ten seconds and spreads a little loving-kindness is to 'wish happiness'. Google pioneer and best-selling author, Chade-Meng Tan describes how to do this to Tim Ferriss for his book, *Tools of Titans*.

When at work, home or out and about, identify someone and just think, 'I wish for you to be happy'. Repeat with a second or third person throughout the day if you wish. Being on the giving end of a kind thought is a happy reward for you.

In *Tools of Titans*, a woman describes how doing this loving-kindness practice once per hour for her work day produced her happiest day at work in seven years. Yes, a total of 80 seconds of wishing others to be happy made the work she detested bearable, even enjoyable, for the first time in many years.

STRATEGY 3 – RANDOM ACTS OF KINDNESS

A fun method to be kind is to practice random acts of kindness. The example often given is to buy a coffee for the person in the line behind you, but you can get lots of ideas from randomactsofkindness.org. You can do this for perfect strangers or for friends, family or work colleagues.

For instance:

- lend out a spare pen
- hold open doors for people
- send a friend a bunch of flowers
- give someone a lovely compliment
- pick up litter at the beach or the park
- offer to take a photo of a group of tourists
- leave some extra coins in the parking meter
- return someone's empty supermarket trolley for them
- provide a glass of water to the package delivery person

Look up 'random acts of kindness' and you will get a multitude of lists you can select ideas from.

It has been proven that doing five acts of kindness in a single day gives a significant boost to happiness.

No Crowbar Needed

Remember, kindness doesn't need to be forced. Put away the crowbar! Get fun back into your life and then not only will your joy bring happiness to others, but you will want to be kind and give back more to the world because you already feel so great.

The next chapter is all about harvesting even more fun from our everyday lives, so turn over for the next ingredient in sparkle: Lightheartedness.

Challenges

Challenge 1 – Practice active listening by not finishing sentences, not changing the subject back to yourself and asking at least two follow up questions or saying "tell me more"

Challenge 2 – Try the loving-kindness practice of wishing happiness silently at least once today

Challenge 3 – Do at least one random act of kindness this week

9

LIGHTHEARTEDNESS

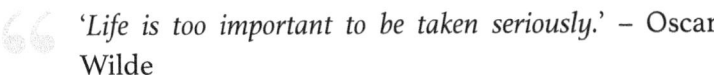'*Life is too important to be taken seriously.*' – Oscar Wilde

DINER EN BLANC

I recently attended the sixth annual Diner en Blanc event here in Auckland. Diner en Blanc involves taking along your own picnic hamper plus small, foldable table, white chairs, white tablecloth and white napkins and then having dinner with thousands of other glamorous strangers all dressed to the nines completely in white at a secret location.

It. Is. So. Much. Fun.

The most common response is a question along the lines of "what is the picnic for?" People enquire if we are raising money for a charitable venture, whether there will be a keynote speaker or if it is part of a business? No, no and no. The Diner en Blanc picnic has been created simply for the participants to enjoy themselves. No other reason. And believe me...

It. Is. So. Much. Fun.

People say arranging to go to Diner en Blanc every year seems like hard work. They would be spot on. As the thousands of guests put in so much effort just to get there, everyone is ready to cut loose and have a grand old time.

It. Is. So. Much. Fun.

I am not saying prioritizing fun is easy. It may take some hard work and organization to participate in even the smallest fun activity, but that only makes the experience richer and more fulfilling.

Play Versus Playful

We have already talked about Play so you may be thinking what more can be added with this element of Lightheartedness? I think of play as an action, something you are doing, something you are using your body for. I think of lightheartedness as being playFUL. It is the mindset side, the BE, not just DO aspect of bringing the sparkle back into your life.

Think of the difference between Play and Lightheartedness as the difference between doing what you love and loving what you do.

Feeling cheerful and carefree when we were kids was easy but now we are all grown up, being serious is our default. Becoming more lighthearted shouldn't be so hard! We think that if we allow ourselves to stop being serious then it will all fall apart. We confuse being carefree with not caring. And we tell ourselves we are too busy or don't know how to be more lighthearted or it is only for children. Check back to Chapter Three for rebuttals to those excuses.

Let's check in on how you are. Right now, unclench your jaw, drop your shoulders and relax your tongue. Were these parts tight? How is all that tension helping us?

We care so deeply it hurts and this has translated to grim living. But we can care AND be lighthearted. Let's find out how...

Lightheartedness Strategies

1. No News
2. I Love That About Me!
3. Lighten Up

Strategy 1 – No News

This powerful suggestion stops negative and harmful thoughts from entering your mind and ruining your day.

Stop watching, reading and listening to the news.

Right now.

Stop the news.

Remove the news apps from your phone, stop the notifications, swap your newspaper with a fluffy magazine, and change the channel when the news comes on. Replace the negative input with a positive, interesting or educational one—a TED talk, a podcast, an audiobook or a funny YouTube clip. You will be amazed at how much more time you have without constant news disruptions and how much more positive you feel when surrounded by upbeat stories.

Switching off the news is not turning a blind eye to the pain and suffering in the world, but it does stop you feeling terrible about it and so adding more weight to it. And it doesn't mean you are 'uninformed'. Headlines will creep into your world regardless of how vigilant you are. Let someone else tell you the latest breaking news; give them the opportunity to inform you what is going on.

Some of you may find this an extraordinary request, but you don't need to know everything that's happening in the world, especially if it makes you feel crappy. The fact is that the news is designed to scare people. It is certainly not there to help us feel cheerful and relaxed. Trying to feel lighthearted while consuming the news is like sunbathing at night – it will never work.

Not consuming the news for a week may be hard but feeling terrible because you watched some horrible, devastating news story that you can do nothing about is even worse.

Strategy 2 – I Love That About Me!

We are our own harshest critics, the chatterbox in our head can be so very mean at times. Our lives never stack up to the Insta-perfect feeds we see. But how to change? Where to start? You have years, decades, of unkindness towards yourself to undo. Why not try this little mantra from author and coach, Jeannette Maw?

I love that about me!

The exclamation point is mandatory.

Isn't this simply fabulous? We are unique individuals with a variety of strengths and weaknesses. We are better at some things and worse at some things. None of us is great at everything. Our diversity is humanity's greatest strength. Let's embrace it.

The best time to use this mantra is when you feel shame, embarrassment or lack at something you can't do well. Instead of denying it, own it with lively exuberance. Just because you are 'bad' at some things doesn't make you any less of a person. Often it leads to hilarious stories and an opportunity for others to help you – i.e.: extend their kindness to you. It also doesn't mean you give up or never try to do that thing better. All it means is that next time you will attempt it with a lighter understanding of yourself.

Examples taken from my own life:

- "I snowboard like a drunken monkey" – I love that about me!
- "My four-year-old can draw better than I can" – I love that about me!
- "I couldn't use a compass to get out of my own house" – I love that about me!

Try it. Next time you find yourself in a position where you are doing something that is not your strength, don't beat yourself up – just say (in your head, muttering, or out loud and proud) – I love that about me!

Strategy 3 – Lighten Up

One way to lighten up is to simply lower your expectations. I am not for an instant saying that you shouldn't strive to be the best person you can be. What I am suggesting is to take action, go for it, proceed and not spend too much time dwelling on the exact outcome you want.

After all, the outcome is unlikely to perfectly match what you expect. Either it falls short of what you desired, in which case you are disappointed or annoyed, OR you exceed what you thought, which makes the outcome you aimed for irrelevant.

When acting lighthearted, remember to choose your environment with care. Funerals, the court room or in airport departures queue may not be the best place to indulge in these fun practices. But please don't use that as an excuse not to attempt to love whatever you are doing.

We live in the most safe and abundant time in human history, the zombie apocalypse hasn't arrived as yet, so let's celebrate being alive!

Here are three actionable ways to lighten up:

Say YES. I know, I told you earlier to say no. I want you to say no when you feel resentment. And I want you to say YES when you may default to a no because you think you are too busy for fun or have some other poor excuse. A while back I was just leaving a friend's house when our two boys asked if they could throw around some water balloons. My default answer was a 'no' as I had to go soon but my friend said 'yes' with the caveat to throw the balloons at the fence outside and not at each other. They followed the rules and had the best time for just a few minutes. The smiles on both their faces were as wide as the sun. If I had defaulted to my usual no because of a perceived lack of time, my son would not have that cherished memory of a few minutes of carefree fun with a friend.

Make up your own rules to bring about joy. Not everything you do is going to translate into the utmost jubilation at all times, but we can learn to be happier with even the most arduous of tasks. As discussed in *Minimalism*, finding ways to transform positive experiences you dislike – especially ones that lead to growth and contribution – into positive experiences you enjoy is the ticket to long term happiness and fulfillment. Author and entrepreneur, Tony Robbins used to hate playing golf as he didn't like all the rules. Now, he loves it because he made up his own rules and goes out to smash the ball around and have a blast with his close friends. How can you make washing dishes or data entry more fun today?

Shake that ass! Put on a song and dance to it. Some call this 'a one-minute dance party'. Speaker and ultimate performance specialist, Joseph McClendon states that when you move your body you change your attitude. He calls this 'asstitude'. Stand up, move your ass and forget about your problems for a few seconds. It's been proven that dancing helps you to rewire your brain into a more productive and happier state. Put some alarms or reminders on your phone to 'shake that ass' today.

These suggestions are just the tip of the iceberg. Find your own ways to lighten up. Embrace 'Talk Like a Pirate' day. Plan a party where everyone wears mullet wigs (as suggested by investor, Chris Sacca in *Tools of Titans*). Tell a silly joke. Or simply give yourself a hug - you will look weird but you will feel good. And remember when you are down that nobody, not a single soul on the planet, can continue to be frustrated while saying 'bubbles' in an angry voice.

Pathway to Joy

Adding fun back into our life allows us to say no to things that are not that important – all the distractions and multi-tasking madness. It helps to clear pathways to what really makes us happy – and isn't that what we want?

Many of us crave something sweet and think we will find it in the back of the pantry or fridge. But this craving for something sweet is not a nutritional need, it is a deep need for more light and laughter in your life. Do something nice for yourself that doesn't involve chocolate: prioritize fun and give yourself the chance to have some sweet and essential joy.

After all, as they say, there is little point of taking life too seriously as none of us make it out alive.

Challenges

Challenge 1 – No news for one week - aim to not watch, listen to or read any news for one week and if your spirits improve, extend the experiment

Challenge 2 – Say "I love that about me!" next time you do something 'wrong' or 'badly'

Challenge 3 – Shake that ass - dance to your favorite upbeat song for one minute and reap the benefits of 'asstitude'

10

EXTRAORDINARY

 'Beauty begins the moment you decide to be yourself.' – Coco Chanel

GRANDMA

My paternal grandmother, Marjorie, was unreservedly and unashamedly my absolute favorite grandparent. Why? Let me tell you about her:

Grandma, despite not being able to finish high school because she had to help out her family, was one of the most intelligent and wise people I have ever met. Until a few months before her passing, she did the crossword puzzle every day. She had a love of books and read prolifically, a love that was passed down to me. It was at Grandma and Granddad's home that I first read the classic, *Little Women* and it was at their home that I read it another half dozen times.

My grandmother was really good-natured, appreciative and grateful of her life. She always said she was thankful for all the simple things – her family, where she lived and the things she had done and seen in her lifetime. After she celebrated her 80th she would say to us: "every day is a bonus."

In addition, Grandma was kind and loving. She spent almost 60 years with Granddad and often said to us: "if he had two heads, I would have married him." We always thought it was funny imagining Granddad with two heads. She would go out of her way to help those less fortunate and was active in various charities and community endeavors. I very rarely heard her say an unkind word about anyone.

I always thought of Grandma as an 'extraordinary-ordinary' human being. She didn't change the world, but with her wise, kind and appreciative traits, she made her little corner of it a great place to be.

Recipe for Sparkle (Again)

Here again is the recipe to help you rediscover your sparkle:

- Mix together savor, play, appreciation, rest, kindness and lightheartedness
- Add a generous dollop of fun, love and energy through suggested strategies
- Bake in some acknowledgement of just how extraordinary you really are
- To create a delicious life you absolutely love

All the sparkle elements and strategies lead to here.

We can now start to accept just how extraordinary we are.

Still not there yet?

You are Extraordinary

Rediscovering your sparkle is primarily about eliminating superfluous stuff from your life to bring you back to what is truly important to you. The sparkle strategies and challenges are ways for you to reconnect with your core self and embrace the extraordinary being that you already are.

Sure, these suggestions are a little uncomfortable as they make you different, make you stand out. But the truth is, you do stand out, as you are already extraordinary.

This is not nonsense.

It is fact.

> **Think about it – you are the only YOU that has ever existed and will ever exist in this world.**

Because we have finally indulged in some much needed ME time, we are able to take a look and assess some of our triggering emotions, bad habits and stories that hold us back. Now that we have boosted ourselves up with giant, delicious helpings of sparkle, we are now able to take a breath and show up. We can do the things we are put on the planet for, take action on the goals that were just buried dreams, travel to that exotic place that has only been a fantasy or work on a long-term project that leans into your purpose.

> **The more you know about who you are, what you love and what drives you, the easier it will be to feel successful and fulfilled.**

The planet and the universe need your special input. We need you to be the mightiest human you can be. The person you are meant to be. But if you are not at the point of striving to reach your potential just yet, know that you don't have to do something extraordinary to be extraordinary. Just deciding to face each day with cheer, to show up, to strive for happiness makes you one of the remarkable few, in a world where default living and stress is the norm. We may have fairly mundane lives, but we can still find joy in the ordinariness.

Despite the world being on fire all around us, we CAN decide to be rebelliously cheerful and content.

Allowing sparkle back into your life will lead you to other important qualities that have fallen away. Creativity, imagination and dreaming big, among other traits, stem from savoring, play, appreciation, rest, kindness and being lighthearted.

So be your unapologetically weird self, whatever that involves. Be quirky, whimsical, wonderful, irreverent, poignant, esoteric, celebratory, funny, honest, loving, joyful, or whatever makes YOU extraordinary.

This is your permission slip to return to your fabulousness. This is your permission slip to allow some jubilation in. This is your permission slip to embrace that inner sparkle.

Be happy or else.

Sparkle Day

There are a number of sparkle strategies and challenges listed in this book and you may be thinking, where do I start? They all seem so delicious but it is stressing me out trying to figure out how to be happier!

Here is my solution: decide that tomorrow will be 'Sparkle Day'. This doesn't replicate all strategies and challenges but creates a combo of the best parts together.

You can select whatever strategies and challenges you want for your own Sparkle Day.

Here is one Sparkle Day itinerary you can apply that incorporates an abundance of fun, love and energy for a small cost and time commitment:

- The evening before Sparkle Day, take all push notifications and news apps off your phone and make a promise to yourself not to check social media more than three times the next day
- As soon as you wake up, thank your bed (giggle optional)
- Meditate for three minutes, taking some slow, deep breaths while you do so
- Bounce out of bed and give yourself a bit of a jiggle and a stretch
- Do a one minute dance party – shake that ass – either now or schedule it in during the day sometime (perhaps after the savoring or gratitude exercises)
- Add an alarm or calendar reminder on your phone so it will go off three times during the day to remind you to stop and 'Take Two' – savor something for two minutes, taking some slow, deep breaths while you do so
- During the day, when you see someone, say in your head 'I wish for you to be happy' – try to do this at least three times
- At the end of day, ask yourself (and your loved ones if they are around) "what are you grateful for?" and "what are you happy about?" and bask in appreciation for a few moments

- Make sure you are in bed, lights out by 10pm – 'catch the 10 o'clock angel train'
- Optional: plan to do 30 minutes of play – something you really love to do – remember this is only 2% of your day

Total time commitment: less than 15 minutes without play or a total of 45 minutes with the play activity.

I don't expect you to aim for a 'Sparkle Day' every day. But I do want you to feel what it's like to live with sparkle for a day, catch hold of the best parts of it and then turn into a habit so that it can enhance your life.

At the start of the book I said that I wanted to create a sparkle movement. Any time you commit to Sparkle Day, get in contact with me and I will do it with you. This is the real start of a movement – two people deliberately striving for something better.

Simply email me: julie@julieschooler.com with the subject line: Sparkle Day.

Dandelions (Again)

Eloise recently turned four. I asked her what she wanted for her birthday breakfast and as we didn't have the ingredients to make what she wanted, I decided on the spot to have a Mama and daughter date at the local café. On our walk there, Eloise got excited, let go of my hand and scooped up a dandelion clock so she could blow the spherical seed head into the air.

My stomach growling, looking ahead at the café in the distance, I hadn't even noticed it.

This time I stopped with her and said, "Remember to make a wish before you blow."

I may not be as effortlessly tapped into my inner sparkle as my young child, but I can sure as heck embrace sparkle when it's on offer.

Our breakfast together was great, but it was this little moment that will be treasured forever.

APPENDIX

CHALLENGES

Savor Challenges

Challenge 1 – Do a digital declutter in any way that benefits you the most, e.g.: remove push notifications, have an email unsubscribe-fest and delete apps that you don't use

Challenge 2 – Each day: 'Take Two'. Take two minutes, three times each day to savor

Challenge 3 – Once this week: listen to a whole album from start to finish

Play Challenges

Challenge 1 – This week: practice saying no, at least once, in the politest way possible

Challenge 2 – Create your 'playlist' - a list of things you would absolutely LOVE to do

Appendix

Challenge 3 – Schedule in a 1 x 30-minute session for play in the next week. Bonus points if you manage 30 minutes per day of play for a whole week

Appreciation Challenges

Challenge 1 – Thank your bed every morning straight after you wake up

Challenge 2 – Choose a gratitude practice and stick to it each day for a week

Challenge 3 – Attempt the massive appreciation exercise once this week

Rest Challenges

Challenge 1 – Breathe – do a deep breathing exercise intermittently throughout each day

Challenge 2 – Meditate – do three minutes of meditation every day for a week

Challenge 3 – Go to bed, lights out by 10pm every night for a week

Kindness Challenges

Challenge 1 – Practice active listening by not finishing sentences, not changing the subject back to yourself and asking at least two follow up questions or saying "tell me more"

Challenge 2 – Try the loving-kindness practice of wishing happiness silently at least once today

Challenge 3 – Do at least one random act of kindness this week

Lightheartedness Challenges

Appendix

Challenge 1 – No news for one week - aim to not watch, listen to or read any news for one week and if your spirits improve, extend the experiment

Challenge 2 – Say "I love that about me!" next time you do something 'wrong' or 'badly'

Challenge 3 – Shake that ass - dance to your favorite upbeat song for one minute and reap the benefits of 'asstitude'

Sparkle Day

Here is one Sparkle Day itinerary you can apply that incorporates an abundance of fun, love and energy for a small cost and time commitment (15 minutes or 45 minutes with play):

- The evening before Sparkle Day, take all push notifications and news apps off your phone and make a promise to yourself not to check social media more than three times the next day
- As soon as you wake up, thank your bed (giggle optional)
- Meditate for three minutes, taking some slow, deep breaths while you do so
- Bounce out of bed and give yourself a bit of a jiggle and a stretch
- Do a one minute dance party – shake that ass – either now or schedule it in during the day sometime (perhaps after the savoring or gratitude exercises)
- Add an alarm or calendar reminder on your phone so it will go off three times during the day to remind you to stop and 'Take Two' – savor something for two minutes, taking some slow, deep breaths while you do so
- During the day, when you see someone, say in your head 'I wish for you to be happy' – try to do this at least three times

Appendix

- At the end of day, ask yourself (and your loved ones if they are around) "what are you grateful for?" and "what are you happy about?" and bask in appreciation for a few moments
- Make sure you are in bed, lights out by 10pm – 'catch the 10 o'clock angel train'
- Optional: plan to do 30 minutes of play – something you really love to do – remember this is only 2% of your day

— A *NOURISH YOUR SOUL* BOOK —

CRAPPY to HAPPY

SHAKE OFF STRESS AND REDISCOVER YOUR MAMA MOJO

JULIE SCHOOLER

CRAPPY TO HAPPY

Shake Off Stress and Rediscover Your Mama Mojo

-A *Nourish Your Soul* Book-

Julie Schooler

1
WHERE HAS THE HAPPY GONE?

 'Life begins at the end of your comfort zone.' – Neale Donald Walsch

COMFORT ZONE OF CRAPPINESS

You have everything you have always dreamed of—healthy kids, a nice home, a loving partner... and you still feel crappy. You bicker with your significant other, snap at the kids (and immediately regret it), and you feel anxious, rushed and overwhelmed every single day.

Life should be amazing, but it is just tolerably mediocre. You feel guilty for wanting it to be awesome, especially when there are millions of people in the world much less fortunate than you. So you reach for the wine, chocolate or television and continue living in your comfort zone of crappiness.

Why do you feel so stressed, worried and angry about your full, busy life when this is what you have always wanted? These constant negative feelings need to stop, but nothing you have tried so far has worked.

This book is full of wisdom from top personal development gurus, positive psychology researchers and families who use these tools every day. It shows how a few simple tweaks to your mindset, language and physiology have the power to take your daily life from **crappy to happy.**

It also cuts through the confusion around meditation, provides compelling reasons why a gratitude practice is a game changer and explains the three tiers to ultimate happiness and fulfillment.

In less than a couple of hours this book gives you dozens of no- or low-cost, easy and practical tips for feeling less stressed, less angry and less worried. It stops your mindless habits that create negative outcomes. You may not believe it now, but you WILL start to feel more calm, positive and full of joy.

You won't need to spend hours searching for information all over the Internet. You will have a clear direction and won't be confused by conflicting advice.

Why This Book Was Written

I am a wife, a mama of two young kids and a lifelong learner of self-help and personal development. And I was sick of feeling stressed, worried and rushed every single day. There just had to be a better way to live. Just because everyone seems to feel the same way doesn't make it right.

So I did what I always do. I read. A lot. After all, I have studied this stuff for years. I have a "shelf-help" library at home. I read books, articles, searched the Internet and even went to motivation and self-improvement seminars.

I have distilled the avalanche of advice into simple and practical tips to help mamas just like you and me find our inner wisdom and remember how to love our lives.

Why have I done this? Because I had to. Surprisingly, I could not find one short, easy, clear, gimmick-free guide just for mamas who should be feeling on the top of the world but are not. We are not that unhappy, certainly not bad enough to seek professional help, but goodness knows we have felt a lot better.

I have written the book that I wanted to read.

Benefits

Just think how great it will be when you look at life with a different perspective and with new positive habits in place. There are benefits in so many areas:

- You have more positive interactions with your children.
- Your kids are happier as you are less irritated and stressed out.
- Your relationship with your partner improves as you become more calm, cheerful and fun.
- You spend less time worrying and more time focusing on life's little everyday miracles.
- The whole world gains from your positive and kind attitude.

Other mamas are happy to recommend this one short, easy-to-read guide. Most say it is refreshing that there is no judgment or criticism of where they are. Instead, it offers simple ways to feel better, even great.

Mamas are excited that there is finally a short book that gives them options to go from crappy to happy in an easy and extremely low-cost manner.

My Promise to You

My promise is that if you use even a couple of the tips in this book, you will feel better, family times will be fun again, and you will give your children the best gift of all—a happy mama.

If you can't have a bit of fun and enjoyment during a time when, yet again, you are tearing your hair out just to get your little ones to put their shoes on each morning, then it is really a sad life indeed. So my promise to you is that not only will this be easy, but also you will also have a bit of a laugh along the way.

What Have You Got to Lose?

Don't let that low level anxiety, that negative emotional state, that underlying crappy feeling continue to be the norm. It is a cruel and unnecessary way to live.

Do not wait another restless night to read this book.

Be the happy mama you want to be—not when the kids are older, but right now. Read this book today, and you will immediately start to feel more relaxed and happy.

Change your focus and change your life.

When do you make time for yourself anymore? Think of reading this book as a low-cost luxury, an easy way to rediscover that sparkle you once had. And know that with this tiny luxury comes a bonus: the wisdom in these pages will help you and your family for the rest of your lives.

2
A LITTLE BIT CRAPPY

 'Don't believe everything you think.'– Allan Lokos

A Typical Morning

Rushing out the door, late for kindergarten yet again, I had to ask my four-year-old son, Dylan, three times to put his shoes on. When there was no attempt to do as requested, I raised my voice, "PUT YOUR SHOES ON NOW!" Earlier, my husband and I had already had a mumbled but heated conversation over packing the same lunch for Dylan: "He should eat something better than honey sandwiches every day"; "Well at least he eats it—and if you don't like it, you make his lunch". As I was strapping our almost two-year-old daughter, Eloise, into the car seat, my mind was turning over the long list of things I wanted to get done. I didn't even realize until later that she had said the word "hand" for the first time.

This is my lovely suburban, first world life, day after day.

And it is not that great.

Actually if I am honest, it is a little bit crappy.

Not enough to really complain about. Certainly not enough to consider seeking professional or medical advice. But every single day does not live up to my expectations.

Like many of you, I have been striving all my life to get to this point. I have the home, the husband, the kids. I have it all! I live beyond the 'happily ever after' of romance novels or fairy tales. I live in the space that no one shows realistically on TV, in movies, in books or on social media. I thought after years of striving to get here, I would be automatically enveloped with a contentedness and happiness I had desired for so long.

But I haven't suddenly and miraculously become relaxed, content and happy. I now realize that I have to work at feeling like that just as I worked at getting the outer stuff I wanted. I now need to match the internal with the external.

I want to live to the higher standard of which I know I am capable. Less irritated, frustrated, tired and overwhelmed. More fun, more loving, more calm and full of energy. I want to be appreciative of my life and how fleeting these years of raising children are.

Less crappy, more happy.

The Answers are Closer than You Think

Emotional states are nebulous concepts, so I wanted to find the most specific, practical and easy ways of achieving them. There is an absolute ton of advice out there, but I wanted to know the best tools for a suburban mama with not much time, not a lot of spare cash lying around and that won't involve travel to Italy, India and Bali. What can I do in my own home to make me feel less crappy?

Actually, the answers turned out to be even closer than my own backyard. It turns out that most of the problems lie in my mind—and thankfully, the answers do, too. Yes, I found I could do a magnificent amount to improve my life just by improving my mindset: my thoughts and feelings that buzz around my little noggin. And so can you.

Of course, changing what food and drink you put in your body, how much sleep you get and how often your body moves is integral and helpful. Sometimes altering your environment by decluttering or changing your work hours can help. But if you want immediate results, then taking a look at your behavior and attitude and examining your mindset are the best things to focus on. In doing so, it may even help you sort out some of those other areas of your life that are not up to par.

You may now be getting annoyed. Not another *The Secret*! I promise you that this book is not a repeat of that book/film. *The Secret* suggests that a new way of thinking could win you the lottery. All I am saying is that by using some of these techniques, you will feel happy even if you never win another penny.

Let's be perfectly clear from the start: if you are feeling angry or sad or overwhelmed in a specific situation, then it is perfectly OK to feel that emotion. Feel it for an appropriate period of time and then move on. More on how to do this later.

This book is about not having to feel that low level irritability, rushed pressure, worry and annoyance every minute of every day.

Just because a generally crappy emotional state is common doesn't mean it is normal or acceptable.

There are ways to break free and feel good, even—dare it be said—great.

I Had to Write this Book

I didn't want to write this book. It felt like I was complaining about nothing. Who am I to write a book about feeling a bit irritated, worried and crappy at times? I have won the golden ticket in life! I have clean running water, healthy children, a roof over my head. More than billions of people can ever dream of.

I didn't want to write this book, but I HAD to. I NEEDED to. This book is waaaaay more personal than I am comfortable with. I didn't want to admit I yell at my kids and argue with my husband. I didn't want to confess how much I long for a wine or two or three each evening. But I had to find some answers and not live this way.

Because if I felt this way, then other mamas probably did, too. So many of us feel crappy day in and day out. Then just to increase our misery, we often like to add a side serving of guilt as we feel a bit crappy about our lives but don't know what to do about it, and therefore do nothing.

If I can help just one mama to feel less anxious on a daily basis, to not lose her temper or to reconnect with her fun side (without the wine), then this book has done its job.

At the very least, she will know she is not alone; there is someone struggling, just like her. Maybe by stepping out of my comfort zone and writing this book, I will encourage a mama or two to step out of theirs and try something new that makes them feel a bit less crappy.

. . .

WHO IS THIS BOOK FOR?

You are a busy mama, so I don't want to waste your time. First up, when I say 'mama' it is an all-encompassing term to mean a mother, stepmother, grandmother, even an involved aunty or friend. Mama is a good synonym for all the different mother terms out there like mom, mommy, momma, mum, mummy, mumma, mother or ma. If you are a mama under any of these titles or definitions, then this book is written especially for you.

Who is this book NOT for? This is not a parenting book. It is not going to tell you the best way to parent a toddler in the middle of a tantrum, a child who doesn't want to eat dinner or a teenager who has lost his manners. Nor is it a relationship book, so it won't tell you how to 'fight right' or negotiate with your partner. But it is meant to help you feel better and often respond better during —or shortly after—these normal everyday situations.

If you are going through a diagnosed medical issue, chronic sickness, a life upheaval or a tragedy, there are more suitable books and resources out there to help you, although the tips in here can help as well. And if you suspect your issues may be coming from a more serious cause—perhaps an undiagnosed mental or physical illness—I don't want to diminish the seriousness of your situation. Please seek appropriate professional advice.

Who is this book really for? This is for those of you who don't want to change your lives as such. You want to keep the external aspects of your life, but you want to feel happier within the life you have created. You want to not yell at the kids or argue with your partner as much. You want to savor a glass of wine with some girlfriends at the end of the week, not gulp it down every night. You want to not feel so rushed, stressed, distracted, tired and annoyed all the time. And although you want things to be different, you want to eliminate the guilt about wanting more when you have so much already.

This may seem too good to be true, but isn't it worth a try? What have you got to lose? These are all low- or no-cost proven methods that you can test out. In fact perhaps the first mindset shift should be from a pessimist viewpoint to an experimental one. Let us act like scientists and test the hypothesis. Let us act like our own children and develop some natural curiosity and wonder around a new concept. Let's embrace some change.

This book is for mamas who are willing to step out of their comfort zones, try a couple of things and take some action. There will be some daily and weekly challenges in the book. Why not try something for a week or a month? This is an insignificant amount of time to decide whether you want to continue with something that has the potential to make you feel amazing.

This All Sounds Good But is it REALLY for Me?

Let's counter some of your top-of-mind objections before we go any further. First, this mindset change may seem 'fake', or you may feel like you are manipulating yourself. Let's try a little experiment. Wherever you are, sit up very straight, shoulders back, like a soldier or the Queen and smile. Smile wide. Smile like your life depends on it.

Do you feel better?

So it feels inauthentic or 'not real', but you feel better? Mmmmm.

Why do you think your current negative thoughts, lousy feelings and mindless habits are more real than positive thoughts and feelings and living mindfully? We will get into this in a big way shortly, but you don't have to believe everything you think.

Put this on your wall:

YOU DON'T HAVE TO BELIEVE EVERYTHING YOU THINK

If a 'truth' is making you feel crappy, isn't it worth exploring an alternative 'truth' that could make you feel great even if you feel 'fake' as you practice it? Don't we all 'fake it until we make it' when learning something new?

You may say, OK, I would give it ago, but it seems like a lot of work. I don't have time. You just don't realize how busy I am. Most of these tips are about changing your thoughts, emotions and language, and this doesn't take much time out of each day. It is mainly about awareness and a little bit of practice. The biggest time commitment is ten minutes of meditation per day. If this seems like a daunting chunk of time to carve out, then start with 16 seconds and work up from there. Yes, 16 seconds. Surely you can spare that?

Isn't it worth a little bit of daily practice to move from crappy to happy? Isn't it worth some effort to stop being so stressed and frantic all the time? Finding ten minutes per day to meditate is hard. Living a crappy life full of tension, worry and stress is hard. You have choices. <u>Choose your hard</u>.

Maybe you think that becoming happier doesn't seem like an important enough goal. It seems frivolous or too self-centered. Sure, you want your kids to be happy, but you? Oh beautiful mama, you are a kindred spirit. Boy do I know this feeling.

You OWE it to your children to be as happy as possible. Not only will it reduce the chances of being irritated and snapping at them, but they also get to see and model a happy mama.

Maybe you feel like you can't possibly ask for more when your life is so blessed already. Actually, to turn that on its head, you OWE it to the world to be happier with the gifts and resources you have been bestowed. Otherwise you have been given the golden ticket and thrown it away.

Lastly, maybe you are worried about how this change is going to affect your loved ones. Are they going to like it? Won't they get annoyed when they can't access mama for ten minutes during her meditation time? Your partner and kids may want to come with you on this journey – they could be as into it as you. Group meditation as a family is an option.

But honestly, if you don't want tell them about this, at least not straight away, your partner and kids may not notice at all. There will be a general lighter feeling around the place, and you will know you have put in the work to create that, but they will just continue on like normal.

If there is a comment or even friction, explain that you are working on becoming nicer and happier for them. Shift the focus back to them. Tell them you are going to be the same mama but more YOU: around more, less distracted, less stressed, happier and more fun. How could anyone say they wouldn't like that? Plus they are your family; they should want the best for you.

If there is still some conflict, realize that their reactions are just coming from their own needs, and you have the power to respond in the most resourceful way you can. Yes, power—more on your personal power very soon.

But before we launch into the solutions, we are going to investigate why we have a tendency to feel unhappy and also why it is worse now than ever before. Yes, it is going to get a whole lot darker before the dawn. On this journey, awareness is as important as action, so let's gets some understanding of the key topics before we launch into the mindset magic.

3

THE DARK NIGHT OF THE SOUL

 'Do one thing every day that scares you.' – Eleanor Roosevelt

Ball of Fear

Eleanor Roosevelt is widely attributed to saying 'Do one thing every day that scares you'. She is considered a wise woman, and I don't want to disrespect her, but I find this advice redundant. I do dozens of things every single day that scare the heck out of me without actually even trying to select one thing.

I am a ball of fear. I worry from the time I wake up in the morning to the time my head hits the pillow. I don't like standing in front of the microwave for fear that it will explode outward or I will slowly get radiation poisoning. Don't get me started on how scary previously innocuous things like driveways, baths and windows are now that I have children.

Even doing something mundane such as filling up the car with gas makes my heart race. I have this vision that as the car is filling up, it will spontaneously explode with my children stuck inside it. Yes, there was a news item on this. It has actually happened (in that case I don't think there was anyone inside the car).

Do you know people have been swallowed into sinkholes as they sat in their own living rooms? Nowhere is safe. My kids have normal things happen to them, and I immediately exaggerate the impact. A small cut will turn to gangrene, a bump on the head is permanent brain damage, a cold is meningitis. I am the best in the world at catastrophizing. The zombie apocalypse could happen any day now.

What are all this fear, worry and anxiety about? Where does it come from?

It comes from The Lizard.

The Lizard

Not a pet lizard, but The Lizard that resides in our brains. We are evolutionarily hardwired for survival. In prehistoric times, we needed a robust flight or fight or freeze mechanism for when we spotted a saber-toothed tiger, or when it spotted us. In our heads is a little area near the brain stem called the amygdala, and it prompts us to constantly scan for anything that can kill us.

In caveman times, anything that could kill us was usually either **scary**—large beasts with sharp teeth, or **scarce**—lack of food, water or shelter. As this is a survival tool from a primitive era, the author, coach, and wise soul, Martha Beck, describes this part of us as 'The Lizard'. Others have called it the chatterbox (Susan Jeffers), the obnoxious roommate (Arianna Huffington), or— excuse the potty mouth—the 'bee-arrcch' (me).

Let's stick with Martha Beck's description for now. The Lizard is a reptilian animal in your brain that perks its head up and alerts you to anything you perceive as scary or scarce. It does this to protect you, but it means your brain is wired to find the negative at all times. It tells you nasty stuff and is generally responsible for all your damaging thoughts, especially critical self-talk.

There are two main points here. First, you must start to think of it, whatever it is, as a separate thing. It is not 'you'. It is a tiny part of your brain pelting you with fearful thoughts and feelings. I repeat, it is not YOU. I like the idea of a lizard since I can picture it in my head. In fact, Martha Beck has a seemingly weird but great suggestion to help with the lizard fear, which I will explain shortly.

The second main point to pick up is that The Lizard tells you things are scary or scarce even if in reality they are neither. It alters your perception. Random sinkholes aside, you, in the Western world, live in one of the most abundant and safe times in human history. As there is nothing really dangerous going on and you have enough to eat, The Lizard turns its attention to other things it thinks you might like to worry about.

> Your Inner Lizard now tells you day in and day out that you lack time, energy, money or love.

Think about that for a moment, instead of being scarce in water, food, shelter and warmth, your Lizard brain is trying to protect you by telling you that time, energy, money or love are scarce and need to be conserved. It is fake fear, but it feels very real. You rush around like you are escaping from a predator, active and alert, but most of the rush is to escape your own worries.

You get an email from your boss saying that he wants you in a meeting in thirty minutes about that project you just handed in.

What does your Inner Lizard say to you? That you must have done a great job and he wants to give you a raise? Doubtful. The Lizard tells you that the project was not up to standard, your reputation is ruined and you are about to be fired.

You get a call from school saying your eldest started a playground scuffle. What do you think first? Is he a bully? I am a terrible mother? He will now never get into college?

Your partner comes home from work and turns the TV on without much of a greeting. Is he angry with you for something or is he simply exhausted? The Lizard likes to make everything personal, even if someone else's behavior has nothing to do with you. It does this to protect you, but in doing so it fills you with negative and fearful thoughts.

The good news is that you can override the Lizard, your primitive alarm system. This book explores many ways to do this, but right now, I encourage you to do what Martha Beck suggests. Go out and buy a representation of a lizard. Anything you can hold in your hands that is a lizard or has a picture of a lizard on it. For example, a notebook, a coffee cup, an ornament or a bracelet. Don't spend too much. Mine is a key ring, and it was a good excuse to shop on Etsy. (I LOVE that online store).

Go on, do it. At least order it. I will wait.

Now that you have ordered it or have it, name it. Yes name it. I named mine Penelope and she is a real bee-arrcch. She tells me all sorts of crappy thoughts and wakes me up at 3am to bombard me with them. Martha Beck recommends this because you now have a physical thing that you can see is outside of you. The Lizard is really not part of you. SHE, Penelope Lizard, is not ME, and so I don't have to take her seriously. When Penelope wakes me up, I tell her that she is being silly. I shush her and tell her to go back to sleep. Works like a charm.

But I am getting ahead of myself. This is not a solutions chapter. This is the dark night of our souls chapter. Let us continue to drag ourselves through the mud and grime.

THE SIX HUMAN NEEDS

Author, coach and personal development expert, Tony Robbins, has popularized the theory that all of us have six human needs. These are needs, not wants. We crave these on a deep level.

We have a need for **certainty**—to feel safe and secure and to know that our expectations will be met. In apparent opposition to this, we have a need for **variety**—to have surprises and spontaneity in our lives (taking a vacation, for example). We also have a need for **significance**—to feel important and that our lives have meaning. On the other side of the coin, we have a need for **love and connection**. We can't be too individual, too significant or we often lose connection with others. These four needs are our core or personality needs.

The other two needs are for **growth** and **contribution**. These are our secondary or spiritual needs, and not everyone gets these two needs met as the other four can take priority. We will delve much more into these two spiritual needs later in the book. This is an extremely concise description, and I encourage every one of you to look up Tony Robbins's explanation of these needs in more detail.

Many people intuitively sense a truth in 'The Six Human Needs'. But you don't even have to believe it. They are needs and they run your life regardless of whether you think they do or not. How you try and meet these needs—in positive, negative or neutral ways—plus which needs you emphasize, have a major impact on your life.

. . .

CERTAINTY

For now, let's concentrate on the need for certainty and how much it pervades our lives. We have a need for certainty because The Lizard craves certainty. The Lizard's main focus is safety, security and comfort, and it likes order and predictability more than anything else. It thinks our lives depend on it, so it tries to control the world around us. And this is helpful, to a degree. Then, as we discussed above, it can be harmful.

At a Tony Robbins seminar I went to recently, about 80% of the 5,000 attendees had the need for certainty at the top of their needs lists if they were honest with themselves. And of the thousands of us who had placed certainty at the top, *every single one of us* desperately wanted certainty to be not as important as the need for love and connection.

We strive for and crave love, but our Inner Lizard behavior leads us instead to certainty.

Think about it, when have you fought with your partner to put your opinion across even though in showing you were right, the relationship was damaged? When have you told your kids they were wrong about something that was not important? Just the other day I had a prolonged argument with my four-year-old about whether Dory was a boy fish or a girl fish. Why do you reply to just one more email to get your inbox in order when you child is waiting for you to play?

You may be annoyed at yourself right now, but remember that this chapter is simply about awareness. Don't judge your past self. After all, not only do you have The Lizard and a frenzied need for certainty to deal with, but also some in-built fears.

TWO MAIN FEARS

All of these thoughts The Inner Lizard tells us boil down to two primary fears that we all have. We fear that we are 'not enough' and as a result won't be loved.

The fear that we are 'not enough' is hard to grasp. Not enough for what, for whom? Susan Jeffers in her classic self-help book, *Feel the Fear and Do it Anyway*, explains that the fear of 'not enough' is the fear that 'I can't handle it'. 'It' in this case being the situation at hand.

We are all hot messes who are constantly told by our Inner Lizards—which are supposed to be there to protect us—that we are not enough and so won't be able to handle our lives and as a result won't be loved. Isn't that depressing and terrible?

As babies we need connection and attachment to survive, but as adults we don't actually need love to live (although it is of course preferred). However, thanks to our Lizards we think we are scarce in the one thing we have the greatest fear about losing—love.

So we often scramble to get love in any form that is offered, even if that is doing more to hurt us. For example, staying in a violent relationship, finding positive emotions from the food we eat, or even in less significant but more prevalent ways like trying to people please in order to avoid feeling rejected.

In other words we often strive for love because The Lizard creates fake fear that tells us that our lives depend on getting love, but often we only get comfort (certainty) instead. These are powerful concepts and they are hard to accept, but please don't dismiss them.

I did warn you it would get darker before the dawn!

Believe me, I also don't want to think of myself as an anxious person driven by a Lizard who seeks out love at any cost, but some of my behavior conveys this so perfectly there is an obvious truth to it.

When, late in the evening, I stand in my dark kitchen bathed in the light of the refrigerator, I have to own up to the fact that the sweet thing I am craving is probably not contained inside it.

Vulnerability

All humans have a Lizard creating a whole lot of fear and a need for certainty. So why now, as mamas, does this seem worse than ever? Why has the worry and anxiety that has accompanied us our whole lives now cranked up the volume?

Yes, of course part of it is that we have taken on more responsibility and so are busier and often more tired. I don't want to underestimate energy and tiredness, they are huge topics (more in later chapters), but I think there is something even more fundamental going on.

I have always felt a bit anxious and worried in life. I mean there is so much that can go wrong, and we hear about disastrous, tragic events on a daily basis. But after I had kids, this low-level worry increased exponentially. Now I have everything I always dreamed of having. And I have MUCH more that can be taken away from me.

Once you have kids, you have some BIG stuff to lose if it all goes wrong. And what is vulnerability but a constant state of UNcertainty? This is exactly where you don't want to be. Brené Brown explained this in her fantastic TED talk on the subject of vulnerability, 'The Power of Vulnerability'.

Go look it up and watch it now. I will wait.

Right, back with me?

When you feel vulnerable and don't like feeling like that, you numb your emotions or you grab for certainty in any area to cope with it. However, you need to simply live with your vulnerability, to own it. I agree with Brené Brown that this is not a state in which I am comfortable. But the next few chapters explain that this is not only possible, but necessary for a happy life.

A Perfect Storm

Between your Lizard brain, the fears that you are not enough and won't be loved, your desperate need for certainty and your extreme vulnerability, it is amazing that you are even able to get out of bed in the morning and function at all!

You have a perfect storm of crappiness!

Beautiful mama, please raise one hand above your head and bend it at the elbow so your hand rests on the back of your shoulder.

Give yourself a pat on the back.

Congratulations, not only do you get out of bed every morning, but also you mother your children with the best resources you have. You are to be commended.

You have also gotten through this chapter, and this is a very hard chapter! Now that you know all this stuff, there is no going back. You have woken up. The first step is awareness, which you have now conquered. Your brain is a tool that you want working for you, not against you. Your thoughts, emotions and hence behaviors and habits are all within your control. Isn't this a great notion? You strive for certainty and it is within you all along.

Dawn has broken.

ALL THE CHAPTERS END WITH CHALLENGES. THESE ARE ALSO LISTED in the Appendix. I urge you to adopt the daily challenges into your life every day for the next 30 days in order to make them into habits. The one week challenges are either tasks for you to do in the next week or experiments to try for seven days to improve your life.

DAILY CHALLENGE – Notice. Start being aware of when your Lizard brings up fake fears and strives for certainty when it doesn't serve you. Do this with curiosity and without judgment.

ONE WEEK CHALLENGE – Buy a lizard. In the next week, buy a representation of your Inner Lizard.

4

MAMA MINDSET: THOUGHTS

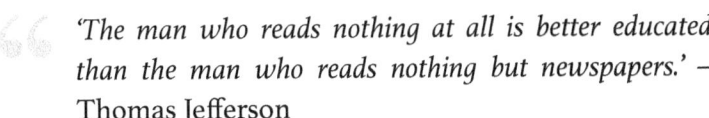 *'The man who reads nothing at all is better educated than the man who reads nothing but newspapers.'* – Thomas Jefferson

THE SIMPLE DIAGRAM THAT WILL CHANGE YOUR LIFE

Please pay attention and study the simple diagram below as it will CHANGE YOUR LIFE. I am not saying these words lightly. This simple arrangement of words has the potential to have a powerful impact on the rest of your life.

Are you ready? Here goes...

SITUATION / CIRCUMSTANCE ->
THOUGHT / MEANING / BELIEF ->
EMOTION / FEELING ->
ACTION / BEHAVIOR ->
OUTCOME

Your life is determined by the meanings you place on external events. Meanings you have decided upon. You decide the meaning. You.

The main thing to realize is that you have the power to control all the components in this diagram between situation and outcome. You often do not have the power over the situation or the outcome, but you can decide on the thoughts, emotions and actions in between. You wanted certainty, and it is right here for the taking. Because you have the control, you have the ability to also change your beliefs, choose your feelings and determine your behavior.

This is best shown with an example.

The Bedtime that Goes on Forever

Almost every night, Dylan, who is nearly five, extends his bedtime in a variety of ways. He will ask for one more book to read together. Or he can't find his pajamas (they are always in the same drawer). Or he finds a toy to play with when it is teeth brushing time. And just when all the bedtime stories, tucking in, and cuddles are finished and I am leaving his room, he wants to tell me one more tidbit of vitally important information about his day, or he insists I kiss his stuffed crocodile or turn the glow light clock towards his bed a little more.

This is a situation or circumstance. In itself it is a neutral thing. A normal everyday occurrence. There could be thousands of different meanings I can attach to this situation, but I habitually return to the same thought most nights. This is often a collection of mostly negative thoughts, along the lines of:

'Why does he always do this? I am hungry. Why can't he just go to bed like other kids? This is my precious time'. The underlying belief here is that Dylan is being disrespectful or ungrateful.

If I am thinking that my beautiful almost-five-year-old son, who just wants to spend a few more minutes with his only Mama is being rude or unappreciative, what do you think the next step—my feelings and emotions—are? Usually it is a toxic cocktail of irritation, frustration and annoyance.

And if I am feeling like that, what do I usually do? A quick, dismissive hug? A rant about how it is my time and I need to go now? An abrupt "It's past your bedtime, goodnight Dylan," and a switching off of the light? Yes, all of these at one time or another have occurred. Sometimes all in the same evening.

What if, for instance, Dylan got into bed a little earlier, I had eaten dinner already and my favorite TV show wasn't going to start for at least half an hour? Perhaps my thoughts about a few extra minutes with my son would be dramatically different. I could think, 'My darling boy, he will be grown up soon and won't want his Mama around so much'. Or I am grateful that we get to spend these few minutes one-on-one without distractions. Overall I would believe that he is showing me love in the best ways he can at his age. I would feel happy, content, grateful. With a couple more hugs, I would turn off the light softly with a whispered "I love you to the moon and back".

I want you to feel, really feel, these two situations in your body. Which of these outcomes feels more pleasant to you? Do you feel tense and tight reading one and lighter reading the other? Which of these is crappy and which of these is happy?

What was the difference between the two? It was not the situation. It was my RESPONSE to the situation. Even the amount of time my reaction would take would be about the same. The difference in the outcome, though, is extraordinary.

But, But, But

BUT you say, I don't have thoughts, I just have feelings. I just get annoyed. Or frustrated. Or worried. Or all of them combined. I argued with my coach for a whole session over this when I first learnt about it. Thoughts, what thoughts? There are no thoughts! My brain is like an IV line to pure emotion.

Let's get this straight. Everyone—you, me, your kids, all of us—have a thought (or many thoughts) BEFORE the feeling or emotion hits. Every time. This thought may be only a whisper, or a belief almost buried at the subconscious level, or such a collective jumble of thoughts that a single cohesive view is hard to pinpoint. But you ALWAYS have a thought before a feeling. Your first job is to become aware of it. Then you can change it.

BUT, you say, even if I did believe you, I could probably change a thought or two, but I certainly can't change my feelings. And even if I wanted to change them, isn't it better to feel your emotions and not suppress them? You have much more control here than you realize. This chapter concentrates on your thoughts and beliefs. More will be revealed about emotions in the next chapter (spoiler alert: it is possible and even OK, depending on the situation, to change them as well).

BUT, you say, even if I decide to go along with this crazy talk, if I change my thoughts and emotions, the outcome may not be what I expect, want or like. And yes, that is completely true. Dylan may still want a story after last cuddles. But you have a better chance of the outcome being more positive and you also have the choice of how to respond to any alternative outcome that comes your way. This is not a one-time special. This is a continual practice that you will get better at.

The extended bedtime situation above doesn't really seem like a big deal. But night after night after night? I really want the last thing my son sees and hears every evening to be a smiling, loving parent who says goodnight gently. I can at least control that part of the outcome.

ANTs

Once you understand that you are in control of your thoughts, once you *really* get it, you will grasp just how powerful this concept is. Even believing that we have control over our thoughts is a belief in itself. Perhaps it is not 'the truth' but isn't it more empowering than the belief that we are simply rag dolls reacting to our environments?

You have approximately 50,000 thoughts a day. (Who counts these things?) Around 80% are both negative and on repeat! Most people are thinking about what they don't want. The psychiatrist, Dr. Daniel Amen, calls these 'Automated Negative Thoughts', ANTs for short. Your mind is swarming with thousands and thousands of ANTs!

Even if you start with only one or two per day, can you see the power of changing a few of your thoughts to new, positive ones? How would that impact your life? Imagine thinking about what you DO want instead of what you don't want.

How do you start? Start with the small things. When you notice a negative feeling or tension as a response to something your kids are doing—not finding their shoes, eating breakfast slowly, making puddles from splashing in the bath—stop for a moment and catch your thought. Grab hold of it (or a bunch of ANTs if it is more than one) and with wonder and curiosity, not judgment, really investigate it. What meaning are you placing on what is happening in the external environment? For instance, they don't care about their belongings, we are going to be late, look at the mess I have to clean up.

Here is the empowering part: just for a moment, switch your meaning to something else, anything else. Could that be a true perspective on the situation as well? Not finding shoes—the shoes are small and pinching their feet or the wrong color so they don't like wearing them. Eating breakfast slowly—they are tired from a late night, or don't like the new cereal. Splashing in the bath—they absolutely love having a bath and splashing is their favorite thing right now. Does the different thought make you feel anything different? Does it make you want to act differently? Don't worry about feelings and behavior right now; all we are doing is playing with alternative thoughts.

Remember, most of your negative thoughts are on repeat. Once you start doing this for a while you will notice patterns in your ANTs. Groups of ANTs stick together and pop up again and again. Usually my individual negative thoughts, although specific to a situation, boil down to 'They are being ungrateful or unappreciative' or 'My time is being wasted' or 'I am too tired to clean up another mess'. The patterns in my thoughts lead directly back to what my Lizard keeps telling me is scarce—love, time and energy.

What does your Lizard repeatedly tell you?

All you need to do now is to become aware and try to change some of the situation specific or little thoughts. Once you practice this for a while, you can start to tackle those patterns of thoughts from your Lizard—your beliefs.

A belief is a feeling of certainty about what something means. It is often something that you have told yourself thousands of times over many years so it can be a bit more 'sticky' and may not change overnight. In order to change it, you have to create certainty around a different meaning—decide to believe another truth. Yes, that could be wrong, too, but isn't it worth experimenting?

Become a mind detective, curious but unbiased. If you are not there yet with all this digging into your subconscious, don't worry, that will come in time. Yes, sometimes it is not fun to look into your deep, dark mind and poke around. I have realized that a lot of my catastrophizing must come from a 'soap opera' mentality that started when I watched *Days of our Lives* with my mother when I had a sick day from school. Remnants of 20-year-old story lines were floating around in my head contributing to my needless worry and everyday angst. As I started to be aware of them, I could simply see them for what they were—made up stories—and let them go.

Tools to Attract a Lighter Thought

I know, I know, you are just beginning to realize that up until now, you have created your own misery. Not the weather, not the economy, not your kids—you. Without awareness, you are driven by your mindless habits. And with your Lizard piping in at every opportunity and all your ANTs swarming over your mind, it is little wonder you haven't been as happy as you would like to be. Please don't add to your negative thoughts by being critical about your past self.

You are blessed with the responsibility to create your own joy. Isn't this wonderful? You have a desperate need for certainty, and you can gain it by taking control of your thoughts.

What are some of the main tools you can use to switch your focus and attract a 'lighter' thought, so you lean into an equally acceptable but happier belief?

The first way, of course, is to notice that the thought originates from your Lizard. Not from you, but from a tiny part of your brain that is rigged to attend to danger. Once you know that The Lizard is not you, then you don't have to take the thought as seriously. Instead of thinking 'I think...', say that 'The Lizard thinks...'. When The Lizard pipes up about something, especially at 3am, tell it to shush and go back to sleep. Treat your Lizard like you would a four-year-old who calls you a poop head. You wouldn't believe that child, so why would you believe your Lizard?

Another way to identify the thoughts is to speak them out loud. This not only slows down the thoughts racing around your brain, but often you realize how silly they are. "He is not putting his shoes on because he is being deliberately naughty" doesn't often stand up when you observe the truth of the situation: he didn't hear me, he is putting his school bag in the car, he can't find them, etc.

Counteract your thought with humor. If you have a recurring belief, especially a negative one about your body, kids or relationship ('I am fat', 'I am a bad mother', 'he doesn't love me enough'), then say it to yourself out loud in a silly voice while looking in the mirror with your finger up your nose. Yes, put your finger up your nose and say it. I guarantee that you will not take that bad, untrue thought seriously ever again.

Question the thought. Ask if that thought is always true in every situation. 'He never listens to me.' Really? Every single time you talk? Question whether the outcome of your thought is actually that bad: 'I always have to run after my kids to round them up for school' could actually mean some extra movement in my day that is good for my body.

REMOVE THE SOURCE

The four tools above reduce harmful thoughts, but this powerful suggestion stops them from entering in the first place. Although The Lizard is responsible for your negative thoughts, you inadvertently keep feeding it every day by adding more bad and destructive inputs mostly in the form of the news.

Stop watching, reading and listening to the news.

Right now.

STOP the news.

Remove the news apps from your phone, stop the notifications, swap your newspaper with a light-hearted magazine, and change the channel when the news comes on. Replace the negative input with a positive or interesting or educational one—a TED talk, a podcast, an audiobook or a funny YouTube clip. You will be amazed at how much more time you have without constant news disruptions and how much more positive you feel when surrounded by upbeat stories.

Turning off the news is not turning a blind eye to the pain and suffering in the world, but it does stop you feeling terrible about it and so adding more weight to it. And it doesn't mean you are 'uninformed'. Headlines will creep into your world regardless of how vigilant you are. Let someone else tell you the latest breaking news; give them the opportunity to tell you what is going on.

Some of you may find this an extraordinary request, but you don't need to know everything that is going on in the world, especially if it makes you feel crappy. Not consuming the news for a week may be hard. Feeling terrible because you watched some horrible, devastating news story that you can do nothing about is hard. Choose your hard.

DAILY CHALLENGE – SHUSH YOUR LIZARD. PRACTICE TELLING your Lizard to shush. When you realize a thought is simply a Lizard opinion that doesn't serve you, tell it to shush and go back to sleep (extra points for saying it out loud).

ONE WEEK CHALLENGE – No news for one week. Aim to not watch, listen to or read any news for one week. Find some TED talks to watch or a new podcast to listen to instead. See if your spirits improve, then extend the experiment.

5

MAMA MINDSET: EMOTIONS

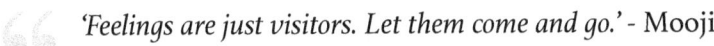 *'Feelings are just visitors. Let them come and go.'* - Mooji

THE CHANGE YOUR LIFE DIAGRAM (AGAIN)

Let's look at the simple 'change your life' diagram again:

SITUATION / CIRCUMSTANCE ->
THOUGHT / MEANING / BELIEF ->
EMOTION / FEELING ->
ACTION / BEHAVIOR ->
OUTCOME

You are practicing changing your thoughts, beliefs and meanings you associate with events in your life and are noticing that this has the power to change your feelings and behavior.

However, emotions are often more powerful than thoughts, so getting them on your side is crucial. Just because a thought can change doesn't mean your feelings align easily. And if you don't align them right, they can easily annihilate any chance of you being happy. So what do you do about your emotions and feelings?

An Emotional Issue

Feelings can be a tricky area to approach as most of us have spent many, many years not dealing well with emotions.

I felt bogged down by an array of negative emotions that I didn't want to acknowledge. My feelings had a lot of power—remember I argued with my coach that I ONLY had feelings, not thoughts? The roar of all my combined emotions frequently drowned out any thoughts and I was left with an overall crappy feeling.

I also wished I didn't FEEL anything at all. So I would stuff my emotions right down and eat a snack, or distract myself with a screen or go shopping... or on a good day I would exercise or bury myself in my work. Of course, sometimes watching TV or exercising or shopping is simply a fun thing to do, but I admit that they have also been habitually used to numb my real feelings. Not feeling much at all can be more preferable than sometimes feeling joyous AND at other times being sad or angry.

Think about what you have done when you felt a crappy emotion. Stress at work? Do you seize hold of your evening glass of wine like your life depends on it? Irritated the towels are on the floor and don't want to nag your partner about it yet again? Switch the TV on. Feeling a bit dejected or rejected? Chocolate fix coming right up.

Maybe you have a different numbing mechanism. Maybe it is a more positive one, like going for a run or having a deep cathartic conversation with a friend—but many of us still don't actually acknowledge and FEEL our feelings. Numbing is so prevalent and normal that it takes some extraordinary perception to even uncover that that is what we are all doing.

> Unacknowledged yet dominant negative emotions need to be brought into line.

It's time to start feeling again, but properly this time. So how do you go about acknowledging your emotions in an appropriate manner, giving them some attention but not being inundated and thus debilitated by them? And what do you do if you don't want to feel that way? How can we all go from crappy to happy in an emotionally agile way?

Fortunately, this is a simple three-step process with a choice at step two of how to deal with the emotion, depending on the situation.

STEP ONE – ACKNOWLEDGE AND LABEL

The first step with emotions is to acknowledge them. This is that awareness concept again. Instead of using wine, TV, chocolate, shopping or even exercise to hide an emotion, accept it. How do you do that?

First, clarify which emotion you are mostly feeling. Label it. Emotions can range from, for example, being slightly irritated to a full throttle rage, with annoyance and anger in between. Or from melancholy to misery along a large spectrum of sadness. So how do you put a label on it easily and quickly?

Author, coach and wise soul, Martha Beck, again comes to the rescue with a fine-tuned method. At any one time, she argues, we are feeling one of four emotions—mad, sad, glad or scared. These are relatively self-explanatory. Mad meaning any of the angry ones, sad being the depressed ones, and scared being the worried, anxious or fearful ones. Glad being what we want more of—happy, happy, joy, joy.

Assign which emotional category best describes what you are currently feeling. Just notice it, validate it, and don't judge yourself for feeling this way. Once you get better at this, you can also notice the intensity of the emotion, but for now just classify it.

Step Two – Feel the Emotion ... or Don't Feel It

You now have a decision whether to feel the emotion or not. You really don't have to feel an emotion every time it appears, but that does not give you a free pass to go back to numbing it. You are making an empowered choice.

The situation or event has a vitally important role here. If you have a death in the family, or you are passed up for a well-deserved promotion, or your child misses her best friend's birthday party because she is unwell, then you have a legitimate reason to feel an emotion. But if you are stuck in traffic again, or your brother forgets your birthday like he always does, or your kids are not coming to the dinner table when you ask, then maybe you don't need to feel an emotion, or at least not feel it so intensely.

If you decide to feel it, then feel where the emotion resides in your body. Is your stomach in knots? Is your jaw tense? Are your shoulders scrunched up to your ears? Do your eyes feel sore and weepy?

> It is called a feeling because you are meant to feel it.

So feel it. Let it move through you. It won't stay in your body forever, except if you try to stuff it down into your little toe. Notice it, give it a label, feel it and let it move through you. Its power will diminish in a shorter time than you think. Once you practice this, just the act of validating and labeling the emotion will decrease the intensity of it.

When you are feeling it, let it out in an appropriate manner. Tell your kids that 'Mama is feeling a little annoyed because we are late again', but don't honk the horn and hit the steering wheel. If your child attempts to run across the road, and you grab him, stop and take a deep breath, then explain that roads can be dangerous and that you were taking a deep breath to steady your nerves and reduce how worried you were. This models to your kids that it is perfectly fine to feel emotions and that they will pass.

On the other side of the coin, you don't have to be ambushed by your emotions. You can choose how you want to feel and then decide on the thought that leads to that feeling, or at the very least choose a less intense negative emotion.

If you are stuck in traffic day after day, what is the point of being annoyed about it or worried what your boss will say? Instead you can feel excited that you get to listen to that podcast episode. Tell your boss that you will make up the time over the lunch break. At the very least you can decide to only feel slightly irritated, not full of immense road rage. You will get to work feeling much more refreshed and productive. Would that be a better start to the day?

It is perfectly acceptable to feel an emotion, but for how long? Should you allow it to diminish on its own accord, or help it to be released? A deep, intense emotion is more likely to stick around than a mild feeling, but we also have some power in this regard.

The personal development master, Tony Robbins, argues under his '90-Second Rule' that whenever you feel like you are in 'a suffering state'—feeling a negative emotion that you no longer want to have—feel it fully for 90 seconds and then get yourself out of it.

Now 90 seconds is not a long time (after all, most of us are not as enlightened as big Tony), and if you are in that state for 90 minutes or 90 hours or even longer, that is acceptable at times, but the concept remains the same. Feeling a bad emotion should be the same as stubbing your toe—intensely painful and all-consuming at first and then fading to less painful so that soon you forget what that pain even felt like.

Give yourself permission to feel the feeling and gracefully let it go. But if it doesn't want to budge, then make a conscious decision not to wallow in the emotion. Move on to happy.

Step Three – Work at Happy

Once the mad, sad or scared emotion has lost most of its energy either through letting it pass through your body, changing your thoughts, or deciding to kick it out after 90 seconds (or longer), your job now is to work to getting the glad emotion back on top. We all lose our cool at times, but how easily and quickly we get it back is more important. Being happy takes work, but what is the alternative? Remember: '<u>Choose Your Hard</u>'.

The aim in step three is to feel more positive, either a little bit or a lot. As Tony Robbins says, move from a 'suffering state' to a 'beautiful state'. Decide to feel better. A more positive frame of mind has an added bonus of improving our creativity and our ability to see other options so we are more likely to find solutions to the problem at hand. Perhaps carpooling, catching the train or working from home are viable alternatives to the traffic issue?

If a move to an ecstatic state seems too hard, try for a one percent improvement in mood. Shift your focus just a tiny bit. There is an arsenal of tools in this book but simple ones to try immediately include taking a deep breath, smiling or looking at a photo of your kids.

As a trial, why not try out the second part of Tony Robbins's 90-Second Rule and completely soak the mind and body in positive emotions? This brief exercise turns up the volume of positive emotions so you flood yourself with them and end up with a higher emotional baseline. It shifts your state from crappy to happy. Remember, you are not replacing the negative with the positive; you are not 'pushing it down'.

> The negative is gracefully released and now you are inviting the positive back in.

First place your hands onto your heart and breathe deeply. Close your eyes if you like. Focus on your heart and breathe slowly into it. Feel its strength and power and miraculous ability to keep you alive and well without you even thinking about it. Ask yourself powerful questions like what are you proud of and grateful for that your (metaphorical) heart has guided you to do? Keep your hands on your heart, take deep breaths and think of three moments from your past (yesterday, five years ago, when you were a child or any time) that make you feel immensely grateful. Fully step into those moments and vividly remember the grace, magic and beauty of the time. Finally, think of one thing you can be joyful about right now. Perhaps your heart beating? The fresh air around you? The beautiful memories you have access to at any moment? Now open your eyes, smile and move on with your day.

In short:

1. Notice, acknowledge, label and validate the emotion
2. Feel it and let it pass OR decide to not feel it, or to not

feel it as intensely by changing your thoughts around it
3. Feel better—slightly or a lot—invite in a more positive feeling

Beautiful State

If this is still too difficult, don't worry. We will delve into both deep breathing and gratitude a lot more in future chapters. This two-minute exercise may be hard work, but it is actually less exhausting and a heck of a lot more fulfilling than carrying all those ANTs and emotional baggage around with you all day, every day.

The more you tap into the happy emotions, the more powerful they become. Focus on joy—being in a 'beautiful state'—and you will experience it even better in the long term.

We have now discussed thoughts and feelings. The next two chapters tackle behavior in the form of physiology and language. Thought it was only a one-way street between your mind and your actions? Think again.

DAILY CHALLENGE – If there is something every day that puts you in a bad emotional state, but is relatively minor (e.g. the traffic, the kids not putting their shoes on, towels on the floor) then practice labeling and feeling the emotion for 90 seconds and then gracefully letting it go.

ONE WEEK CHALLENGE – At least once in the next week try the 'flood with positive emotions' exercise. With your hand on your heart, breathe deeply, feel immense gratitude for particular moments in your life, and think of something you can be joyful about right now.

6
PHYSIOLOGY: THE BODY SHORTCUT

 'That breath you just took...that's a gift.' – Rob Bell

THE BASICS

Perhaps you are not yet convinced of the power of the mind, but luckily for you there is a shortcut to changing your life. Your body, your own physiology. You don't even have to believe positive change is possible (although it helps).

The body has its own mechanisms for making you feel less stressed, more energetic and happier. Think about it for a second —your body wants the best for you; it wants you to be physically and mentally healthy. You need to listen to it and tap into its innate wisdom.

Until now, this book has put aside some of the basics to getting your life back on track. You are more likely to snap at the kids or your partner or make poor food choices if you are tired or hungry. Everyone knows that quality food, sleep and movement are essentials for better living, and indeed make us happier, but as busy mamas these seem like lofty goals.

I am not for one minute underestimating how important these basics are, but they are not the focus of this book. There are entire books dedicated to healthy diets, getting better sleep and moving your body. This chapter is a quick overview to remind you of their importance, but I urge you to seek out guidance in the areas that particularly resonate with you.

TIRED ALL THE TIME

Many busy mamas feel tired all the time. As my own mother has said to me, "You were born and I never slept soundly again".

Changing your mindset and how you treat your body is a great start, but if you are living healthily and still feel chronically tired, then it is worth seeking professional help. You may have an underlying thyroid, hormonal, adrenal or another issue that is not being picked up. At the very least, I suggest you read my coach, Louise Thompson's book: *The Busy Woman's Guide to High Energy Happiness* or nutritional guru, Dr. Libby Weaver's *Exhausted to Energized*.

Regardless of whether you seek further guidance from books or professionals, it is worth trying to get some of the following basics right first. These have a significant impact on your energy levels.

BREATHING

Many negative thoughts bounce around in our heads without us being aware of them. Some of our beliefs are buried so deep they are ingrained in us. We may be able to grab some of the conscious thoughts and beliefs and start choosing to switch them, but what about those ones down in the abyss of our subconscious? The most accessible and direct way to tune into the subconscious is through breathing.

We have about 20,000 opportunities each and every day to boost our health and happiness—every single time we breathe. Remember those 50,000 thoughts per day? If you are counting, that's twice as many (mostly negative) thoughts entering our bodies each day as breaths!

Breathing. That thing that sustains life. The ONLY thing we have to do from minute to minute. Breathing.

And most of us DO IT WRONG.

Most people breathe shallowly, only using the upper parts of their lungs. This type of breathing keeps you in your sympathetic nervous system (SNS) and hence holds you in fight or flight mode. Essentially, you are on alert, and your Lizard is ready to inform you of perceived danger at any moment.

It's time to relearn how to do slow, deep belly breathing. Yes, relearn—it is how babies naturally breathe. These belly, or diaphragmatic breaths invoke your parasympathetic nervous system (PNS) and hence your rest, digest and repair systems. Your body slows down and starts healing. When the PNS is active, the SNS cannot be dominant, which means it is more difficult to be on alert and stressed.

Every time you concentrate on slow, deep belly breathing and get your PNS prevailing, your breath communicates to your body and your subconscious that you are safe. That feeling of certainty you crave? You can get it instantly by focusing on your breathing. You have a free, readily accessible, ultra-quick method for feeling less stress and more certainty whenever you want.

Breathe in through your nose and count to four so that your stomach gets inflated, like you are filling up a balloon. Hold that breath for a count of four. Then breathe out through your nose or mouth to a count of four and hold it for another count of four. Don't worry about the nose/mouth thing—do whatever comes naturally to you. Also, don't worry about how many seconds you take with the inwards and outwards breaths and holding it. Just make sure your stomach gets inflated, which means that your lungs are filling up with oxygen.

This is meditation teacher and wellness expert, Davidji's '16-Second Meditation'. I know you are busy, but you have 16 seconds to spare, don't you? Do this as much as you can during the day as a mini reboot to the present. I find it helps to connect it with other daily activities like waiting for the tea to brew, showering and while I am reading in bed before lights out.

Did you know that some people get 'email apnea' while reading their emails? They essentially stop breathing altogether when checking their inboxes as this is a prime time for the SNS to be dominant (ALERT—email danger ahead!). Aim to associate deep, belly breaths with checking emails. If your inbox is as crowded as mine, you will activate the PNS often if you create this mental link.

As Arianna Huffington says in her fabulous book, *Thrive,* the breath has a sacredness to it. One 16-second meditation of focused breathing can transform chaotic energy to stillness. Try to encourage your kids to do it next time they are up to no good. There is often a palpable shift in the room.

If you don't do anything else from this book, promise me that you will relearn how to breathe right.

> Do your own version of the 16-second meditation every day.

Vitality Shortcuts

Although being tired is important to address, there are times when allowing ourselves to fall victim to our tiredness does not help us. I am talking about when you decide to not go to the gym or for a walk because you are too exhausted, or you don't want to get off the couch and play with your kids because you lack energy, or you reply to some emails at work rather than tackling that more mentally difficult job.

In these instances, it is worth trying a few of the tips below to see if you can change your state and hence your weary feeling. Sometimes movement and play is exactly what the body is crying out for. Of course, also go to bed earlier to restore your underlying energy reserves, and if that is not helping, seek expert guidance, but these are worth a try.

Yes, it may seem fake or artificial at first, but an active state of the body often generates energy. These are examples of how the body and your actions can impact your thoughts and emotions. It is a two-way street.

Tip 1 – WATER

Get up, go to the kitchen and pour yourself a large glass of water. Look out the window and feel thankful that you are easily able to access clean drinking water. Drink the water, enjoy.

Tip 2 – YOGA

Do a few sun salutations, or yoga movements that involve the downward dog pose. Look it up if you don't know it. For the very tired, simply lie on the floor with your feet up a wall. These stretch the body and give it a chance to be in a restorative state for a few moments.

Tip 3 – SMILE

We did a form of this exercise at the start of the book. Wherever you are, sit or stand with a straight posture, put your shoulders back and move your mouth into a wide smile. How you feel can determine your behavior, but on the other side of the coin emotion is created by motion. Alternatively, watch or read something for a few minutes that makes you laugh—cat videos, comedians (I recommend Michael McIntyre), misheard song lyrics, autocorrected texts, silly jokes. Laugh heartily. Even a few minutes a day of this 'best medicine' has its benefits.

Tip 4 – DANCE

It was past 10pm on a Saturday evening, and 5,000 completely sober strangers and I had been at Tony Robbins' 'Unleash the Power Within' seminar for 12 hours straight. Every single one of us was dancing like his or her life depended on it. At the front of the room, Tony, a man in his 50s, recovering from injury and disease, was dancing the hardest of us all. I have never seen anyone so vibrant in my life.

Get a taste of extreme vitality through dance. Put on something upbeat and dance for one minute (or more). Your kids will LOVE doing this with you. Dance like no one is watching. Dance like your life depends on it. Dance because your life does actually depend on it.

. . .

The MUCHO MAMA MOJO Challenge

Here is a super duper way to improve the basics that your body craves. These actions will help to uplift your mood, restore your mojo and start to transform your life.

You can attempt one of them in a week, but if you're willing to accept the 'MUCHO MAMA MOJO Challenge', dive in the deep end and do all five. Make sure you choose your week carefully. Don't do the challenge if you have to work late every night or there is a big party on the weekend.

Note that this is not everything your body needs. Less screen time, less caffeine, less sugar and more strength training are some of the other basics that can help you, but keeping it at five makes it manageable and easy to remember.

1. PLANTS – Significantly increase your vegetable intake. For many of us, this means **double** the amount of plant food (non-starchy vegetables) you currently eat each day. The best way to do this is to make sure your lunch and dinner meals are half vegetables, plus add a green smoothie into your day.
2. WATER – Significantly increase your water intake. For many of us, this means **double** the amount of water you drink per day. Most people are chronically dehydrated and don't even know it. Aim for two to three liters, 60 to 100 ounces, 8 to 12 glasses each day.
3. NO BOOZE – No alcohol for one week. This includes the weekend.
4. MOVEMENT – Go for a ten-minute walk outside once a day for a week. The benefits of movement and sunshine for your body and your mood cannot be underestimated.
5. SLEEP – Go to bed, lights out by 10pm every night for a

week. This includes the weekend. Author Marci Shimoff calls this "catching the 10 o'clock angel train". I LOVE that phrase. If you want to read a book in bed, go to bed even earlier.

THE MUCHO MAMA MOJO DOUBLE GUARANTEE:

1. After completing the MUCHO MAMA MOJO Challenge for one week, you will feel healthier and happier. If you don't feel even 1% better, feel free to return this book for a full refund.
2. If you contact me to say you are planning to do a MUCHO MAMA MOJO week (all of these five challenges in one week) I will do it with you. That way I get to support another mama and boost my wellbeing at the same time.

Your physiology can clearly help counter the negativity. It is now time to turn your attention to language and how that can be a hindrance or a help.

DAILY CHALLENGE – DEEP, SLOW BELLY BREATHING—THE 16-Second Meditation.

ONE WEEK CHALLENGE – The MUCHO MAMA MOJO Challenge.

7

LANGUAGE: YOU TALKIN' TO ME?

 'Speak only if it improves upon the silence.'– Mahatma Gandhi

STICKS AND STONES

You already know that your Inner Lizard talks to you all day and all night. It says some nasty stuff, horrible things that you would never say to a friend. You have learned that this is not you saying this, and you can now shush your Lizard, tell it that its comments are not needed or warranted. However, it can still say things that sting. This shows you how much power language has over you.

Whether in your head, out loud or spoken to others, the language you use can have a powerful effect on how happy you are. In fact, if your mindset and body are in line, but your language isn't, it's unlikely you will achieve what you desire.

STORY

Humans are primed for a compelling narrative. Storytelling tradition has been around much longer than the written word. We like to find patterns in events, to see conflict resolved and to have a beginning, middle and end to journeys and situations.

It is time to start paying attention to the stories you tell yourself and others, and also the stories they tell you (or don't tell you as the case may be). Just like you don't have to believe every thought that goes through your head, the stories you tell yourself may also be made up, even though you may behave as though they are the truth.

What do we say to each other when we catch up with friends? Something along the lines of "work—so stressful at the moment, new boss" and the reply: "got given an extra project, been working late, so busy". We take solace in the 'fact' that everyone is rushing around. We are all so stressed and busy, busy and stressed! No wonder we need that wine.

Why would we make these things up? We do it to protect ourselves. The story is a breaker switch to protect us from fear. It protects us, but also imprisons us. If we rush around and tell each other we are stressed and busy it stops us from examining our emotions too deeply, which feels yuck, or it helps us to blame others for our lifestyles so we can eliminate any responsibility to make our lives better. There is always an excuse that stops us from getting what we really want when we live in our stories.

The Language of Emotion

We also tend to blow things out of proportion, exaggerate and catastrophize things. This is essential in a Hollywood film, but there is no reason we need to be so dramatic in our own lives. This is especially prevalent in our language of emotion.

Perhaps because we are so good at hiding our feelings, we only acknowledge when an intense, all-consuming emotion sucker punches us.

How you describe your feelings can increase or reduce their power. Maybe they aren't worthy of such a passionate portrayal. If that car cuts you off, maybe you are 'a bit peeved' rather than 'really pissed off'. If your kid is knocked over in the school playground, perhaps you feel 'a little worried' rather than 'scared out of my wits'. Still feel your emotions, but let the intensity go through you a bit and think before you voice the language around how you are feeling.

THE LANGUAGE OF DISEMPOWERMENT

We use a lot of negative sounding words: 'must', 'have to', 'need to' and that perennial mama favorite 'should' that imply that we don't have options in our lives. This is a language of disempowerment, of exhausted mamas who have forgotten that they have choices. We need to first be aware of this and then STOP it. Immediately.

Another one is the begrudging "yes" when you really mean "no". A polite no response to school committees, family members, friends and of course your own kids is a practice that needs to be firmly in place. As author and entrepreneur, Derek Sivers, says: "If you're not saying 'HELL YEAH!' about something, say 'no'".

Find replacement words that are empowering and say them instead. Here are some positive switches to start you off:

- Must, Have to, Need to, Should -> Could
- Can't -> Won't
- Problem -> Opportunity

- Hope -> Know
- Begrudging 'Yes' -> Polite 'No'

Try this for a week. Simply don't say those negative words. Your Lizard might still think them, but don't say them. Replace the words with more empowering ones. I doubt anyone will notice as they are too busy rushing around being stressed. But you will feel a difference.

IDENTITY

You don't achieve your goals; you get what you believe you are—your identity. This is a powerful concept and not easily grasped on first hearing it. There is a danger to the identity cloak you put on, but it also conveys great influence.

Your identity is not as fixed as you like to believe. But just because you are aware that you can change some parts of your identity doesn't mean you will do it. Your identity brings with it a degree of certainty and security, and you now know how much you need that.

However, sometimes the pain associated with your current identity is so great that you are motivated to find a better identity. I had hated running since I was young and believed I was terrible at it. When it was pointed out to me that this was simply an identity I had identified with, I trained for and completed a half-marathon within a matter of months.

We notice what our identities are when we use 'I am...' phrases. 'I am' are two of the most powerful words in the English language and should be used with great care to craft the identity you want. If you repeatedly say 'I am a procrastinator' or 'I am always running late' or 'I am not a morning person', do you think these are helpful to living a fulfilling life?

Notice when you use 'I am' and ask yourself if it is really true. Especially when The Lizard pipes up and says things to you like 'I am fat'. Really? Are you entirely made up of fat? Are you just fat and nothing else? Perhaps you hold a little more weight around the middle than you would like, but you are not, by the full definition, fat. This questioning of your current 'I am' statements is an interesting exercise.

If you want to take this even further, change some of your 'I am' statements to more resourceful ones, whether they are 'true' or not. When I did this exercise at a motivational seminar back in 2008, I wrote 'I am a published writer and best-selling author' without any thought of how this would ever come about. Occasionally I read that phrase amongst other true statements on my 'I am' list. Today this is a reality for me. The power of the brain astounds me.

Empowering Questions

Most of us have heard about the power of affirmations—repeating positive statements out loud, writing them down or reading them over and over. That 'I am' exercise above is an example of that. Busy mamas don't have time to even think of affirmations, let alone say, read or write them again and again. It feels a little forced.

What can you do instead? Well just like the start of this paragraph, you can use questions in a more powerful way. Using empowering questions has been found to have a greater impact on outcomes than affirmations because if a question is asked, even if it is not spoken aloud, your mind is still compelled to answer it.

For instance, if you are late again, you can ask yourself 'Why am I always late all the time?' or you can think of a better question, for example 'What could I do to not be late to Tuesday's school pick up?' Instead of asking 'What do I have to get done today?' (notice the 'have to'?), say to yourself 'What are the two items I could tick off today that are the most worthwhile use of my time?' Okay, that is a bit wordy, but you get the idea.

We have now addressed the basics around your mind, body and language. The next few chapters take us up a level and crank out the happiness boosters. If you only read one other chapter in the book, make it the next one. The delicious duo of meditation and gratitude have the potential to vastly improve your life.

DAILY CHALLENGE – FIND SOMETHING YOU WANT TO IDENTIFY with and create an 'I am' statement around it. Write it down and read it each day. The best way to do this is to take a photo of the written 'I am' sentence and then make it the wallpaper or front screen on your phone.

ONE WEEK CHALLENGE – Replace all the disempowering words you say out loud for one week.

8
THE DELICIOUS DUO: MEDITATION AND GRATITUDE

 'All of man's difficulties are caused by his inability to sit, quietly, in a room by himself.' – Blaise Pascal

The Delicious Duo

If you don't take anything else away from this book, please give the two tools in this chapter a good try. Both practices in this delicious duo are readily available at any time and are free (or very low cost). You don't even have to believe they will improve your life. Do them every day for a month and you will notice that you feel calmer and more appreciative.

These cornerstone habits create an environment of abundance, not the scarcity your Lizard keeps harping on about.

What are these miracle cures?

Meditation and gratitude.

. . .

Meditation

Meditation is an ancient practice dating back thousands of years. It has been around for millennia because it works. Maybe you tried it but felt like the imperative to clear away all your thoughts was too hard. Or you couldn't commit to an hour a day. Or you didn't know if you were doing it 'properly'. So after a time you stopped.

Now that you have kids, you have been told meditation is even more important, but it seems like just another thing on the long 'To Do' list that you will never cross off.

The Mama Meditation described below is a quick and easy habit to get into. You don't put brushing your teeth on your To Do list, and you don't need to put Mama Meditation there, either.

Meditation Myth Busting

You do NOT have to clear away your thoughts. This is totally impossible. Those 50,000 or so ANTs (automated negative thoughts) may be reduced slightly by a constant meditation practice, but you will still have thousands of thoughts zipping around your brain. Your job in meditation is to observe your thoughts and let them go by without judgment. More on this in a moment.

You do NOT have to commit more time than you can fit in to meditate each day. The benefits of meditation have been shown with a practice that takes as little as three minutes per day. The challenge in this book is to set aside ten minutes per day (or at least build up to ten minutes). Meditating every day is the most important thing.

You can't meditate 'wrong' unless you are checking Facebook or driving or mowing the lawn while you are doing it. For a traditional meditation practice, a quiet space where you are unlikely to be interrupted for a few minutes is the ideal, but even that is negotiable.

Your subjective experience of the meditation is not that important. You may feel bored, fidgety and that you have tons of thoughts, but you still may be in a deep meditation without realizing it.

Why Meditate?

You are already attempting to become aware of your thoughts and feelings. This is a backdoor method through the subconscious to master your mind by quieting it. The point of traditional mediation is to give your mind a rest. A constant practice will calm the mind and leave some space between those thousands of thoughts. Less chatter means a clearer head, a more focused mind and more energy.

Numerous studies have shown a direct link between a consistent meditation practice (even a few minutes each day) and almost every positive health and wellbeing outcome you can think of. It has a beneficial impact on medical issues like nausea, ulcers, anxiety, even diabetes and heart disease. It has lowered pain intensity and decreased the length of the common cold. It has been shown to boost positive emotions like compassion and reduce negative ones such as loneliness in the elderly and post-traumatic stress in veterans.

Meditation actually changes brain function and can help with focus, creativity and maintaining longer periods of productivity. No wonder modern workplaces are embracing it.

If you want to 'get something out' of meditation like it is some sort of transaction, then spend some more time investigating the myriad of benefits it offers. But remember there is no competition when it comes to meditation. Your own practice may improve over time, but the only 'winners' are those who commit to it every day.

> Think of meditation as a little daily luxury, an easy treat, something you can do just for you.

Give yourself permission to do nothing for ten minutes. This sacred ten-minute ritual will help you to be better in all other areas of your life.

TRADITIONAL MEDITATION HOW TO

Your daily challenge is to do ten minutes of 'traditional' meditation. Don't stress about having to do meditation—it is about reducing your stress! You don't 'have to' do it. You are choosing to do it. Find a meditation practice that you like and will keep doing. This may take some experimenting, and this is fine.

First find a quiet place where you won't be disturbed. My favorite place is in my bed, but alternatives are in the parked car, in the wardrobe, or in the bathroom (!).

Find a good time each day when you can meditate around the same time. Favorite times with mamas are in bed before getting up in the morning or last thing at night, in the parked car before they go into work or after the kids go to bed but before they check emails, tidy the house or watch TV.

It doesn't matter whether you sit up or lie down. You don't have to sit in a certain posture or lie in a particular way. You don't have to wear anything special or light candles or anything. Sit or lie so you are comfortable. If you think you may fall asleep, that is fine, especially for a nighttime meditation. If you don't want to fall asleep, then set an alarm to go off at the end of the ten minutes.

In order to let your thoughts drift through your mind many meditation practices encourage concentrating on something in the present. One such thing is the breath, so you can concentrate on your breath going in and out.

Another way to concentrate on the present is to adopt a mantra. This can be linked to the breath, for example, in breath—peace, out breath—calm. At the start, your thoughts will override this practice almost every second, and all you do is get back on track again and again: 'Oh that is a thought about the laundry, breathe in peace, breathe out calm'.

Alternatively, there are guided meditations you can follow. These can cost a little bit of money and will require headphones, but may make accessing meditation and committing to each day easier. You can find guided meditations all over the Internet or you can buy CDs or MP3s of them or download meditation apps. One popular app is Headspace.

The best thing about a guided meditation is that you can concentrate on the music or voice and not the chatter in your head. And even if you don't listen to it 100%, even if you feel your mind drift, you will still get a lot of the benefit of meditation from relaxing and breathing deeply. Believe me, I don't like spending time in my head with all its Lizard thoughts and ANTs. I have found guided meditations the easiest way to commit to a meditation practice each day as someone else's voice, or meditation music is in there instead.

I recommend sorting out a daily meditation practice that works for you. After a while, you can invite your partner and kids to do it with you. It could end up being a sacred and powerful family ritual. But if you can, try to meditate by yourself, at least at first.

My Current Meditation Practice

I have downloaded some of my favorite guided meditations onto an iPod that only has meditations on it that I keep by my bed. I try to wake up and meditate before the kids wake, but if they are already awake I plunk them in front of the TV and their toys (don't judge!) and go back to bed.

I lie flat on my back under the covers then choose a meditation track and listen to it. Most of the downloaded meditations are ten or twenty minutes long. If I think I will fall back asleep, I set an alarm. I concentrate on doing some deep belly breathing. At the end of the meditation I turn off the iPod and the alarm, thank my bed and get up. It is a luxurious way to start the day and always puts me in a better frame of mind.

Please accept the daily challenge at the end of this chapter to meditate for ten minutes per day.

Gratitude

Those of you who are very astute may have noticed that when I finish my morning meditation and before I get up, I thank my bed. I got this tip from Louise Hay, motivational author and founder of the publisher, Hay House. Thanking my bed is both ridiculous and profound. Ridiculous as I am thanking an inanimate object. I get a little giggle from doing it, which puts me in a great mood. It is also profound as I realize how fortunate I am to be sleeping on a bed each night. Most things that are worth pursuing—having kids, for example—are both ridiculous and profound.

I also thank my bed because it is a good way to start the day. Like many things in life, particular care should be taken with the start and end of things, with take offs and landings, and thanking your bed is a good way to 'take off'.

Endings are important, too. (They have done colonoscopy studies to prove this, but believe me, you don't want to know the details.) That is why many of the gratitude practices that are suggested below happen in the evening, although any time of day is good. Just like meditation, find a time of day and a practice that you can stick to and do it every day. It is the everyday nature of it that is important, not what you do, how long it takes or even what your responses are.

The Benefits of Gratitude

Being grateful creates awareness of the good in your life and invites in some more positive thoughts that will start to nudge out some of the 50,000 negative ones. Being grateful for the small miracles of daily life—the super computer in your back pocket, the sunshine on your face, your child's laughter—makes you feel like you have enough, that your world is abundant, not lacking. Insufficient appreciation of the good events of your life and over-emphasis of bad ones are two culprits that undermine contentment. Living in a state of gratitude is a gateway to grace.

Gratitude studies have shown that an appreciation practice is associated with being more enthusiastic about life, being interested in the community, being kinder to others and getting better sleep. One study found participants were 25% happier after only a short time of practicing gratitude. What else could you possibly do to improve your happiness by 25%? (Actually, there is an exercise in the next chapter that also gives this outcome.)

. . .

A Mama's Guide to Gratitude

For mamas, a daily practice is recommended. Unlike meditation you don't even need ten minutes. You can fit it into the daily routine without it taking up any extra time.

At breakfast, in the car on the way to or from school, at dinner time or when the kids are tucked up in bed, before lights out, ask them the following two questions. Answer them yourself as well:

- What are you grateful for?
- What are you happy about?

Kids as young as two or three often get the concept. I don't know why these two questions work well together, but they do. Often I say something more profound, life affirming or esoteric for my grateful answer (the sun, clean running water, healthy kids, etc.). Then I respond with something more ridiculous or materialistic or frivolous for the happy one (my favorite TV program, chocolate or a new podcast I have discovered). You can list many things or settle on one.

My son Dylan, who is nearly five and has been doing this for two years, often says the same thing for both or gets really silly and says things like 'sausages'. The answers are not important, the practice and the redirection of thoughts is.

This practice takes less than a minute out of your day and gives you something to talk about with your kids. Just try it.

You can also cultivate your own gratitude practice. Some mamas like writing a list of three, five or more things they are grateful for each day. Journaling them makes them seem more permanent and real. Again, it is the act that is important rather than what you write.

Many families create gratitude rituals. For example, putting a sheet of paper on the fridge that everyone can add a gratitude item to, or at the Sunday night dinner speaking your appreciation to others at the table.

> Find something that resonates with you and start your own family gratitude tradition.

At dinner time we now pause for a moment and say thank you before we tuck in (similar to saying grace). It is important to remind ourselves of the efforts and resources it takes to bring all this food to the table. From the farmers and land owners who grow the produce to the logistical operations it takes to get it to the store. For the appliances and electricity or gas inside our homes to cook it. And, of course, for the efforts of the chef. We live in a time and a place where food is fresh, varied and abundant, and that is something for which I can easily give my profound thanks.

GRATITUDE WHEN IT IS DIFFICULT

When out and about thank the people who make your day a little easier. Say thanks to the bus driver. Look at your waitress and thank her for her excellent service. Smile at the gas station attendant. Your day is better because these people do their jobs. Saying thanks to others shows your kids that saying thank you is important and valued.

But what if they are aren't doing their jobs well or they are acting poorly? Even more reason to be thankful. You can always find something kind to say to someone, and people who are in a hurt or unresourceful state need it even more than most. They are unlikely to be nice back, but if you are nice to them, you interrupt their patterns of putting negativity out into the world and getting only negativity in return. You can be happy—and thankful—that you are building up your integrity muscle, living to a higher standard by treating people well even when they treat you poorly. Be genuine in your thanks, but just try it with someone who is steamed up and watch their reaction with curiosity.

Once you start to practice gratitude it can get easier. But it is especially important to try and be grateful when things are hard. Marci Shimoff, author of *Happy for No Reason* suggests trying 'brightsiding':

1. Identify a difficult situation you are encountering.
2. List three things you are grateful for about that situation.
3. Find one thing, no matter how small, that is humorous about what's happening.

For instance, you have been on hold to the bank call center for twenty minutes. You are grateful that you have a cordless phone so you can stack the dishwasher while you wait, that you have money in the bank in the first place and that you are not on hold for two hours like you were with the mobile phone company the other day. And the hold music is hilariously horrendous—some sort of bagpipe and pan flute concoction. Brightsiding is exactly how it sounds; it prevents you from feeling anxious and annoyed.

Practice this delicious duo of meditation and gratitude every day and your life will improve immeasurably. You do not need to read the rest of the book. I mean it. Don't read the rest of this book. Just meditate and be thankful. Don't turn the page!

DAILY CHALLENGE – MEDITATE FOR TEN MINUTES EVERY DAY. Start with three minutes and build up if you need to.

ONE WEEK CHALLENGE – Each day for a week ask the kids what they are grateful for and what are they happy about. Listen to their answers and don't forget to answer the questions as well.

9
HAPPY 1.0 – A PLEASANT LIFE

> *'Too much of a good thing can be wonderful.'* – Mae West

Rebel Mama

Hey, didn't I tell you not to turn the page? Wow, you must really want to be happy! Or maybe you have to finish something once you start it. Or maybe you are a rebel mama. Whatever the reason, you are going to love, love, love the next three chapters.

We have become so accustomed to living in our comfort zones of crappiness that we have forgotten what being happy is all about. We see our kids laugh and play so easily and feel bewildered about how they can be so carefree. Then we disregard it as a child thing, not for responsible adults. We have to be serious (look at that language—'have to').

How do you climb out of this pit of despair? Where do you even start? Positive psychologists, researchers whose focus is happiness and other positive emotional states, describe three tiers to happiness: living a pleasurable life, a good life and a meaningful life. The next three chapters tackle what these tiers of living a fulfilling life mean in the real world for a busy mama.

You do not have to take on every suggestion here, but the more effort you put into practicing being happy in all its forms, the more you will get out of it. Remember you <u>choose your hard</u>. You decided to have kids and that is not necessarily the easiest road to take, but ultimately it is likely to be very rewarding.

Attempting these steps to happiness, especially the harder ones, is worth it. But I am getting ahead of myself. First, let's dive into what positive psychologists call living a pleasurable life.

Basking

When I was growing up, we were fortunate to have a swimming pool. We were the most popular house in the neighborhood in summertime! I remember long, long summer days when I was nine or ten years old when the neighborhood kids, my sister and I would swim in our pool then get out and lay on the driveway to feel the warmth of the hot concrete on our backs and the sun on our bodies.

Once we were completely dry again we would jump back into the pool and then repeat the cycle. (This was the 1980s and parental supervision and sun awareness were not as top of mind back then.) That feeling of the warmth soaking into my body still stays with me 30 years later.

>We utterly, completely, enthusiastically basked.

The word 'bask' has two main definitions, and in this nostalgic trip above, we literally basked under the first definition: 'to relax in a pleasant warmth'. But we also basked under its second definition: 'to take pleasure or derive enjoyment' (Merriam-Webster Dictionary).

Basking, or its synonyms, luxuriating, reveling, marveling, relishing or savoring are easy methods of finding pleasure in everyday moments.

> But no one, not even children, basks any more.
> It is a lost art.

Why don't we? We are constantly distracted by our phones, rushed by our hectic schedules, future focused and want to 'save time'. These are cultural constructs that we don't have to buy into. Saving time, for instance. What does that even mean? What do we 'save' it for?

Due to our prehistoric survival instincts, humans are good at building brain structure from negative experiences but poor at doing the same with positive.

To help our minds we need to take a few more seconds to install the positive bits. We need to savor, marvel, bask, to slow down so our brains have time to take in the pleasure and override our natural bias to the negative.

A Pleasant Life in the Present

Everyone should try to stop and smell the roses occasionally, and there are many very good opportunities each day—most of which only take a few seconds—to be more mindful and live fully in the present.

Mindfulness is a trendy concept these days, but it simply means bringing your attention to the present moment. The proven benefits of it are exceptional. It is linked to improved focus, better performance at work, more positive emotions, increased self-knowledge, higher self-control and greater empathy plus all those health benefits with which meditation is associated.

There are many opportunities to be mindful. At work, look up from your computer and focus on something far away, preferably out the window, for a few seconds. This has the added bonus of keeping your eye muscles functioning well.

When you are with your kids and they want you to look at something—a rock, a bug, a fallen branch—stop and really look at it. This also shows your kids that you can give them your undivided attention.

When you are in the car and an old favorite song comes on, really listen to it, turn it up, sing along. With your partner, spend one minute each day gazing into each other's eyes. This may seem weird at first, but it works a charm to keeping the romance alive. Just try it.

In Gretchen Rubin's book *The Happiness Project*, she pauses to watch her kids sleeping for a few moments each evening, a habit she beautifully describes as 'gazing lovingly'. If that is not basking, I don't know what is.

Being mindful can be adapted to many different activities. Simply be fully present and focused on the activity at hand. Yes, this can be hard for a busy, multi-tasking mama, but it's worth trying out to gain the health and happiness benefits noted earlier. Cooking, gardening, walking and playing with the kids are all great ways to try out mindfulness.

Remember each day to pause so that your brain can grab hold of the positive. Soak in the beauty all around you. The more you do this, the more you realize that this is available to do at any time. As Arianna Huffington says in *Thrive*: "The engine of mindfulness is always going. To reap the benefits of it, all we have to do is become present and pay attention."

A Pleasant Life in the Future

You can still live a pleasurable life even if you are future oriented. Studies have proven that looking forward to experiences creates almost as much happiness as the experience itself. This seems to only apply to experiences and not material purchases. Improve your happiness today by savoring the positive expectations of a future experience. I know with kids that sometimes the best laid plans may have to be cancelled last minute, but that doesn't necessarily counter the days, weeks or months of happy anticipation you already had.

Plan a vacation, a weekend away, a night out or a fun family outing. Going to a concert is a good example, as usually you have to book months in advance to secure a ticket. Mark it on your calendar. Tell people you are looking forward to it. Research what you are going to do, wear, eat and drink.

No one has yet proven that money, career choice or—unbelievably—even health, have much of an effect on happiness. But consistently, across many different studies, personal connections and strong social bonds have been shown time and again to make a meaningful contribution to happiness. Luckily for us mamas, we have some tiny humans to look after, a family unit that in theory is shown to be linked to being happy.

A future-oriented way to create a pleasurable life is to create some family traditions to look forward to. Perhaps the start of summer means an evening picnic in the backyard and mid-winter means a special occasion dinner with the nice plates and napkins. Our family looks forward to public holidays, not only as a day off but because my husband makes pancakes for breakfast.

A Pleasant Life in the Past

If you haven't planned anything to look forward to and still rush through your days without pausing to marvel, then you can still gain pleasure from looking at the past.

Create a 'memory jar' with your kids. When you've done a fun activity together, write a little note about it on a small piece of paper and pop it in the jar. I started this for Dylan when he turned four, and we don't do it for every outing or fun activity, but when we remember I write a note and he puts it in the jar. The whole jar will go in his keepsake box and he will be able to read it when he is older.

Positive psychologists have devised a simple but powerful exercise called 'Three Good Things'. Doing this three-minute exercise once a day for one week has been shown to increase your level of happiness by 25% **six months later.**

THREE GOOD THINGS:

1. List ONE good or happy thing from your day.
2. Write it down, tell your partner or speak the answer out loud to yourself.
3. Ask yourself WHY it happened—what was it about YOU (your character, personality, traits, strengths, qualities or skills, etc.) that helped it to occur.
4. Take a few moments to feel good about yourself—SAVOR that positive feeling.
5. Do this whole exercise again for TWO more things if you have time.

For example, there was a beautiful clear blue sky today. The reason this is good is that I am learning to be mindful and appreciate the environment around me more.

It is not the good thing that is important but the connection to you, that third step, that makes this an amped up tool. Step three focuses on your role in creating that good thing and so gets you thinking about specific positive traits in you that contributed to the happy moment.

Over time you see that you have control over creating these happy experiences, and your positive outlook starts to be imbedded in your identity. So you get to feed your need for certainty and transform your identity, two of the most powerful drivers of your life. The savoring step simply locks in all the goodness from the whole exercise.

Try this with your kids at dinner time or bedtime (tack it on the end of a gratitude exercise) or with your partner when you get into bed at night.

These are just a few examples of past, present and future techniques that start to give a sense of living a pleasurable life. As they say, the days are long but the years are short, so commit to enjoying the pleasures so readily available in your life, especially the precious moments with your tiny humans.

DAILY CHALLENGE – DO SOMETHING EVERY DAY THAT involves basking. For example, look out the window instead of the computer screen for a minute, sing loudly to an old song or gaze lovingly at your children sleeping.

ONE WEEK CHALLENGE – Do the 'Three Good Things' Exercise every evening for one week.

10

HAPPY 2.0 – A GOOD LIFE

 'Dying is easy; comedy is hard.' – Edmund Gwenn

HAPPY IS HARD WORK

Although all the exercises in this book so far are designed to not take too much time out of your day, are free or low cost and are proven to make you genuinely happier, they still take some effort, which may of course put you off trying them.

But that is exactly the point! Being happier is HARDER than not being happy. As the ANTs (automatic negative thoughts) crawl over your mind, your Lizard tells you everything is either scarce or scary, and fear leads the way, it is EASIER to complain, grumble, and be discontent.

> It is actually LESS selfish to act happy—it takes determination and discipline.

Unfortunately, our society has a belief that if a person is happy, then they are born that way or find it easy to be joyful, when in fact it usually takes a lot of work.

Mamas, luckily, do not shy away from hard work, so I have faith that you will take the concepts in this and the following chapter on board and work towards being even happier.

Look, I understand if you want to stop at Happy 1.0, but you may as well read this short chapter and see if you want to upgrade now or in the future to Happy 2.0.

Gratifications and Growth

Although the pleasures in life—especially if you are mindful of them—will give you a pleasurable life, there is another level that gives you 'a good life'. This is where you use your strengths and abilities to work towards something, create something or improve yourself. Positive psychologists call these 'gratifications'. It is often linked to a concept of 'flow', which will be discussed below.

A few chapters back we discussed the four primary needs, including the need for certainty. But there are two secondary needs that often get diminished in the compulsion for the other needs.

However, they are absolutely crucial for living a fulfilling life in a 'beautiful state'. One of these is 'growth'. The personal development concept of the need for growth and positive psychologist view of living a good life through gratifications are essentially describing the same thing.

Flow

Can you remember a time when you were completely absorbed in a project or activity? Maybe when you were building something with Lego as a kid, or learning to water-ski or concentrating on a tricky spreadsheet in your work cubicle. The task required concentration and ability that was just at or above your current level, so you were neither bored nor frustrated.

It doesn't matter what the task is. Time seems to pass by quickly, and the outside world disappears for a few minutes or a few hours. This is the concept of 'flow'. We need this to ultimately feel happy, as being in flow is a prime way of expanding ourselves. We gain skills, achieve goals and feel in control while in flow, which leads to growth. Just from the description, it is evident that this is a harder but more fulfilling way to attain happiness in a Happy 2.0 way.

The ironic thing about flow is that while you are in it, you don't actually have an emotional response. You are not in a flow state and also thinking 'boy am I happy', you are just in flow. So, paradoxically, sometimes to be happy you have to find a way to have an emotionless state.

You are certainly not in a flow state if you are distracted, bored or anxious, or all three. And guess what becoming a parent often means? Yes, you guessed it, huge doses of alternating or simultaneous distraction, boredom and anxiety. No wonder we are not happy as mamas; we have huge roadblocks to finding the flow state.

Think about it, your previous avenues for gratification (using your strengths to grow) such as uninterrupted work, an outside hobby or time alone are severely reduced or changed. So you have to find new ways or really embrace the limited opportunities you have to get flow.

I am not for a second saying having kids means an end to happiness. They lead to an overall sense of joy, but in a nebulous kind of way. We also want and need to claw back happiness in specific situations.

Ways to Flow and Grow

One easy way to find your flow state is to simply play and spend time with your kids. I notice that I can be in a flow state while building my own Lego construction and coloring in a coloring book.

New ways of achieving flow states can include parenting related tasks, such as sorting photos into a digital or physical album or editing the videos you take of the kids into a mini movie. (Remember to do a task that is at or just above your level so you don't get frustrated or bored.) This has a bonus that you produce a creation that you can gain happiness from by gifting to others or looking at for years to come.

If you can spare an hour or two a week, it has been proven that couples feel more attracted to each other when they regularly engage in novel and exciting activities that involve working together to achieve a goal. So find something to do with your partner like building a tree house, dancing lessons or improving your chess game.

Committing to doing something for yourself once per week for one hour (e.g. a singing lesson, a yoga class or a painting workshop), will lead you to being a better person in other areas of your life. It adds a dimension of growth.

Sometimes a weekly commitment is too hard and occasional one-off projects are a better fit. A big project carried through to the end in a relatively short space of time can also aid growth and therefore happiness. When I participated in National Novel Writing Month (NaNoWriMo) last November, writing 50,000 words (equivalent of a 200-page book) in a month seemed daunting, but it was in fact a massive happiness boost. It doesn't matter that the silly romance novel I wrote is sitting in the proverbial bottom drawer and is unlikely to be published, at least not in its current form. If you like writing, I can't recommend it highly enough. It ticks all the gratification boxes—flow and growth—that lead to one Happy 2.0 mama.

Perhaps dedicating your limited time to finding your flow state, growing and hence gaining some happiness is not a compelling enough argument. So I will offer you another reason why striving for Happy 2.0 is important.

In order to meet others' needs (like your own kids), you HAVE to grow. Growth leads to giving, which leads to more growth, and therefore more needs are met. You going to that singing/yoga/art class benefits your children, not to mention the entire community! This makes a nice segue into the Happy 3.0 factor—living a meaningful life through contribution.

DAILY CHALLENGE – TRY TO ATTAIN A FLOW STATE EACH DAY, if only for a few minutes.

ONE WEEK CHALLENGE – Start a hobby, project or activity that extends you physically or mentally for a minimum of one hour per week.

11
HAPPY 3.0 – A MEANINGFUL LIFE

> *'The best way to cheer yourself up is to try to cheer somebody else up.'* – Mark Twain

IT'S DECISION TIME

Again, you are at a crossroad and can 'choose your hard'. Being happy is hard, being unhappy when you don't have to be is also hard. As Tony Robbins describes it, you can decide to live in a 'suffering state' or a 'beautiful state'. Of course there is a lot of pain in the world, and living in a 'beautiful state' is not a denial of that pain. It simply removes the link between pain and suffering.

It is your decision—crappy or happy?

And nowhere is that decision more important than in this chapter.

Choosing to be a person who embraces the Happy 3.0 philosophy below takes the most energy, time and work of all of the recommendations in this book, but it ultimately leads to a top level of happiness that most people cannot fathom.

The aim is not only live a pleasurable life or good life but a **meaningful** life. You attain a meaningful life from a connection to a wider cause. In other words, by fulfilling your need for contribution. The positive psychologists and personal development gurus have intersected here again, both with an emphasis on giving.

Give Selfishly

We are told that giving to others makes us happier. Apparently, to be happy, we must give our joy out to the universe freely and abundantly. Except as mamas, we give and give and give to our kids, our families and others, and quite frankly a lot of the time we don't feel great about it.

So why am I telling you to give when you do so much already? You are naturally inclined to provide for others, so change your mindset so you actually start enjoying it. You are a mama and would give the shirt off your back to anyone who asks, so do it with grace and humor. Give without being a martyr about it. Give because you expect to feel awesome and happy because you are contributing.

Give selfishly!

Giving selfishly is not for one instant giving with the expectation that you will get anything back. It is not a trade or barter. All it means is you give knowing you are already gaining more than the person you are giving to in terms of a Happy 3.0 boost.

When you contribute with a selfish altruism, you feel connected to the abundance of the Universe, not the scarcity that The Lizard tells you about.

You give because you know your happiness counts, and if you are happy then others are more likely to be. You give because it takes you into an area of flow and growth.

You give because it grants you a richer life.

Although you are giving 'selfishly' to make your life more meaningful, giving takes you out of yourself, which is another ironic way of gaining happiness. When you make something personal when it is not, for example, bad traffic or the weather, it is a surefire way to be miserable. When you stop relating external stuff to yourself—it is simply the traffic being the traffic—you are choosing a more neutral way of viewing the world.

Taking the 'me' away also helps remind you that you really have no real problems! The traffic does not seem as big a deal when you spend some time volunteering at a children's hospital or a homeless shelter.

Give from the Saucer

Although it helps to view giving in a different way, it doesn't just take a change of mindset to give graciously. You also need to feel fulfilled yourself before you give. This is Happy 3.0 for a reason. Fill yourself up with the other happiness habits first and then attempt this top tier recommendation.

Remember to do some deep belly breaths each day, meditate, express gratitude, savor life's pleasures and give time over to tasks or hobbies that put you in flow and help you to grow. Only after all that is it a good idea to give more than you do already.

As speaker and author, Lisa Nichols, eloquently describes it, fill your cup up so that it is overflowing onto the saucer and only then "serve" from your saucer.

A Life of Service

Practice serving on a small scale. You have already started this with your gratitude practice by giving thanks more freely. Up this with giving information, praise and compliments.

One easy, free way to give more is to listen to others. Like basking, listening is a lost art. Practice active listening. Let the other person finish what they want to say, without interrupting or finishing their sentences. Look them in the eye and act interested. Then ask them at least two follow up questions about what they are talking about without relating it back to yourself at all.

This is especially important with kids who often don't feel heard. They show you a new drawing and point excitedly to the globs of paint explaining what the picture is about. Once they have finished, you can ask them any number of questions like why they chose a particular color, how long it took or where you want to put it when you get home.

Once you get better at these small acts of giving you can consider giving in the form of the two heavy hitters—time and money, mostly in the form of volunteering and giving to charity. Volunteering has the same type of benefits associated with meditation and mindfulness. It is like a wonder drug that improves health, mood and relationships in those wonderful people who volunteer even a little.

Take your older kids to volunteer once a month, quarter or year. Get your young children to help you sort out their old toys to give to a charity. Encourage your children to put aside some of their pocket money to give to a favorite non-profit of their choice. Invite the kids into the kitchen to ice the cupcakes you bake for a local rest home or fire station. Start sponsoring a child in another country and have your kids exchange letters so they can see there is a whole other world out there and hopefully feel fortunate for the life they have.

I have just started helping at Dylan's school for one hour a week. The new entrant classes are scheduled to do specific physical activities that improve co-ordination and motor development, which is made easier when parents assist the teachers.

This makes me feel great as I spend a little extra time with Dylan, get to know the teachers better and feel good by helping the local community. It ticks all my 'giving selfishly' boxes in one go. I am very much 'serving from my saucer'.

If this seems a bit too hard, a fun way to fulfill the need for contribution is to practice random acts of kindness. The example often given is to buy a coffee for the person in the line behind you, but you can get lots of ideas from randomactsofkindness.org. For instance, offer a glass of water to the package delivery person, leave some extra coins in the parking meter or send a friend a bunch of flowers out of the blue. It has been proven that doing five acts of kindness in a single day gives a significant boost to happiness—maybe a new idea to try out as a family?

This chapter is just a taster, a few ideas to get you interested in the concept of giving and contribution so you see the potential it has for connection to a wider cause and hence a more meaningful life.

Remember to fill your cup first, but I hope each and every one of you has a chance to feel the grace and magnificence that occurs when you are able to give from your saucer.

. . .

DAILY CHALLENGE – Practice active listening including not finishing sentences, not changing the subject back to yourself and asking at least two follow up questions with your kids, partner or others at least once per day.

ONE WEEK CHALLENGE – Do one random act of kindness every day for a week.

12

A LIFE OF LOVE

 'To live is so startling it leaves little time for anything else.' – Emily Dickinson

HAPPY VERSUS LOVE

You may be wondering why this book has emphasized happiness over love. Love has been mentioned, but it is happy that this book has highlighted. This is because you already OWN the love part of the equation. You have a ton of love inside you. You did before you became a mama, and now it is infused even more so into your being. The abundance of love is not the problem.

The problem has been your old conditioning, your innate fears and your Inner Lizard driving you. The issue has been a lack of awareness that you can calm the mind, control your thoughts and decide to be grateful and happy in any situation.

CERTAINTY VERSUS LOVE

You have prioritized your need for certainty over your need for love as you have associated the vulnerability that comes with loving wholeheartedly as uncomfortable, even painful. Love can hurt.

Brené Brown says in the 'Power of Vulnerability' TED talk that she is not the kind of person to surrender to vulnerability. And goodness knows, neither am I. I am still very attached to certainty —it has kept me safe all these years. However, it is obvious that the need for love must come first.

> She is trying to live in love, and so can I.
> So can you, if you want to.

When you take deep belly breaths, practice gratitude and meditation, and seek ways to be mindful, grow and contribute, you invite love and joy into your life. You don't have to do everything. Please don't even try. Start with a commitment to one new tool and build up from there.

Basking in Love

After a while you start to get an occasional glimpse that this whole-hearted loving, this state of grace, has been within you all along. You don't have to create it, you certainly don't need to pursue it, you simply need to remember how to get back to that natural state in which your soul feels nourished.

Your life will still be as busy and full as ever, but you will be able to stop and listen to the whispers of your inner wisdom more often. You may even be able to bask in its warm glow occasionally.

But if not, even if you, like me, snap at the kids, bicker with your partner, reach desperately for the wine at the end of the day, know that tomorrow is another day and that you can choose to allow it in then.

Get on the 10 o'clock angel train, and then wake up knowing that you deserve every kindness and you are a wonderful mama.

Lift your head out of this book, take a long, slow, deep, belly breath and smile. Now, go and find that tiny human and give her an enormous hug. Overload him with smoochy kisses. Tell those beautiful children of yours that you love them to the moon and back and always will.

APPENDIX – Daily and One Week Challenges

Daily Challenges

I urge you to try to adopt daily challenges into your life every day for the next 30 days in order for them to become habits.

Notice. Start being aware of when your Inner Lizard brings up fake fears and strives for certainty when it doesn't serve you. Do this with curiosity and without judgment.

Shush your Lizard – Practice telling your Lizard to shush. When you realize a thought is simply a Lizard opinion that doesn't serve you, tell it to shush and go back to sleep (extra points for saying it out loud).

If there is something every day that puts you in a bad emotional state but is relatively minor (e.g.: traffic, the kids not putting their shoes on, towels on the floor), then practice labeling and feeling the emotion for 90 seconds and then gracefully letting it go.

Deep, slow belly breathing—the 16-Second Meditation.

Find something you want to identify with and create an 'I am' statement around it. Write it down and read it each day. The best way to do this is to take a photo of the written 'I am' sentence and then make it the wallpaper or front screen on your phone.

Meditate for ten minutes every day. If you need to, start with three minutes and build up.

Do something every day that involves basking. For example, look out the window instead of the computer screen for a minute, sing loudly to an old song or gaze lovingly at your children sleeping.

Appendix

Try to attain a flow state each day, if only for a few minutes.

Practice active listening, including not finishing sentences, not changing the subject back to yourself and asking at least two follow up questions with your kids, partner or others at least once per day.

One Week Challenges

The one week challenges are either tasks for you to do in the next week or experiments to try for seven days that will improve your life.

Buy a representation of your Inner Lizard.

No news for one week. Aim to not watch, listen to or read any news for one week. Find some TED talks or a new podcast to listen to instead. See if your spirits improve, then extend the experiment.

At least once in the next week try the 'flood with positive emotions' exercise. With your hand on your heart, breathe deeply, feel immense gratitude for particular moments in your life and think of something you can be joyful about right now.

The MUCHO MAMA MOJO Challenge:

1. PLANTS – Significantly increase your vegetable intake. For many of us, this means double the amount of plant food (non-starchy vegetables) you currently eat each day. The best way to do this is to make sure your lunch and dinner meals are half vegetables plus add a green smoothie into your day.
2. WATER - Significantly increase your water intake. For

many of us, this means double the amount of water you drink per day. Most people are chronically dehydrated and don't even know it. Aim for two to three liters, 60 to 100 ounces, 8 to 12 glasses each day.

3. NO BOOZE – No alcohol for one week. This includes the weekend.
4. MOVEMENT – Go for a ten-minute walk outside once a day for a week. The benefits of movement and sunshine for your body and your mood cannot be underestimated.
5. SLEEP – Go to bed, lights out by 10pm every night for a week. This includes the weekend. Author, Marci Shimoff calls this "catching the 10 o'clock angel train". I LOVE that phrase. If you want to read a book in bed, go to bed even earlier.

Replace all the disempowering words you say out loud for one week. For example:

- Must, Have to, Need to, Should -> Could
- Can't -> Won't
- Problem -> Opportunity
- Hope -> Know
- Begrudging 'Yes' -> Polite 'No'

Each day for a week ask the kids what they are grateful for and what are they happy about. Listen to their answers and don't forget to answer the questions as well.

- What are you grateful for?
- What are you happy about?

Do the 'Three Good Things' Exercise every evening for one week:

1. List ONE good or happy thing from your day.

2. Write it down, tell your partner or speak the answer out loud to yourself.
3. Ask yourself WHY it happened. What was it about YOU (your character, personality, traits, strengths, qualities or skills, etc.) that helped it to occur.
4. Take a few moments to feel good about yourself—SAVOR that positive feeling.
5. Do this whole exercise again for TWO more things if you have time.

Start a hobby, project or activity that extends you physically or mentally for a minimum of one hour per week.

Do one random act of kindness every day for a week. Look at randomactsofkindness.org for ideas.

—A NOURISH YOUR SOUL BOOK—

EMBRACE YOUR AWESOMENESS

FEEL IN CONTROL AND BE YOUR BEST SELF IN THIS BANANA-PANTS CRAZY WORLD

JULIE SCHOOLER

EMBRACE YOUR AWESOMENESS

Feel in Control and Be Your Best Self
in this Banana-Pants Crazy World

-A *Nourish Your Soul* Book-

Julie Schooler

1
ARE YOU HOMESICK FOR YOURSELF?

> 'To be yourself in a world that is constantly trying to make you something else is the greatest accomplishment.'
> – Ralph Waldo Emerson

IT'S TIME TO REMEMBER JUST HOW AWESOME YOU REALLY ARE...

- Know how to eat, exercise and sleep well but just don't do it?
- Are you feeling overwhelmed and out of control every single day?
- Want to be more assertive and confident but don't want to appear unkind?

This book gets to the heart of why we know what to do to have an amazing life but stop ourselves from being fulfilled and successful. It delves deep into why we are ridiculously busy, easily distracted and not reaching our true potential. And it provides answers as to why we don't go to bed on time, ask for a promotion and say 'no'.

The latest wisdom from researchers, self-help experts and prosperous, happy people cuts through the confusion around stepping out of your comfort zone, provides compelling reasons for how habits can beat procrastination and explains how to stop worrying what others think.

This is a clear, uplifting guide that will immediately help anyone who is struggling with day-to-day life in this banana-pants crazy world.

WATCH OUT FOR HAZARDS

My bestseller, *Rediscover Your Sparkle*, provides 'sparkle strategies' to fill your cup back up so you can face every day with a smile. And my book for mamas, *Crappy to Happy,* gives step-by-step guidance on how to overcome negative thought patterns, deal with emotions and reach all three tiers of happiness.

After writing those two books, I wondered what more could possibly be written on the topic of living your best life. The conscious act of getting honest with myself and admitting my life still didn't stack up to my expectations made this book take shape. I still get angry and shout. A lot. I often don't think the nicest things about my body. And I can get swept away by worry about my family, friends, finances and this banana-pants crazy world we call home.

Embrace Your Awesomeness builds and expands on these two books and is also fantastic to read on its own. It details four main types of hazardous thinking that prevented me and potentially prevent you from being our best selves: perfectionism, procrastination, people pleasing and playing small. Then it directly explains how to eliminate and minimize these hazards with an 'awesomeness makeover'. You will learn how to increase your self-worth, speak up without fear of criticism and find shortcuts to feel more in control.

I thought about not writing this book as I have certainly not mastered all this stuff myself yet. But then I would be going against exactly what this book is about: stepping out of your comfort zone, being authentic and creating new work regardless of the outcome.

Again, I have written the book I want to read.

I hope you come with me on this journey to start living a truly outstanding life.

BENEFITS

Follow the short, chunked down chapters in *Embrace Your Awesomeness* to:

- Stop being homesick for your deeper self
- Bust myths around willpower and motivation
- Act confidently even if you have low self-esteem
- Love yourself even though that may sound excruciating
- Use simple daily rituals to feel in control in this uncertain time
- Learn how to overcome perfectionism, procrastination and people pleasing
- Feel like you are living the life you were meant to live, one with excitement, meaning and true joy

Simple, Subtle and So Worthwhile

Writing this book and putting into practice these concepts has led to a deeper bond with my husband, an innate confidence in my ability to tackle anything from parenting to business, and a transformation in my relationship with my body.

Life is much simpler than we are led to believe. The changes seem subtle, the concepts are almost intangible, but these really are the most important things. They are what make life worth living.

Ready for profound advice wrapped in a few laughs?

If you take even a pinch of wisdom from this book, it is guaranteed that you will feel in control, thrive in a banana-pants crazy world and give yourself the best gift of all—reaching your true potential.

Embrace Your Awesomeness Today

Where could eliminating exhaustion, resentment and guilt from your life lead? Imagine being at your absolute optimum no matter what. What's stopping you from embracing your awesomeness today?

It's time to get out of your own way.

Read this book and step into the power and brilliance that you know you have deep inside.

2
IT'S NOW OR NEVER

 'Today you are You, that is truer than true. There is no one alive who is Youer than You.' – Dr. Seuss

THE QUARANTINE BLUES

As I write this book, the world is in the middle of the largest global pandemic we have seen in our lifetimes. This invisible plague has impacted everyone. People all over the globe have lost their jobs, their health and their lives. The virus that has swept the world has driven dramatic changes in how we work, live and interact with others.

I am one of the lucky ones. My family and I are healthy, we still have a roof over our heads and food on the table each day. But if you had told me at the start of this year that all the travel I had planned would be cancelled, I wouldn't be allowed to walk along my favorite beach, I would have to homeschool my children and couldn't hug people I loved, I would have laughed at the absurdity of it all.

But here we are.

Stuck at home with my family for weeks on end meant I couldn't fall back on my usual distractions of travel, shopping and socializing. I could be entertained by dozens of funny memes, binge-watch the next big thing or doom scroll the latest pandemic updates, but all that gets dull after a while. Yes, the kids need me and I can always enjoy a good book, but if the fundamentals aren't right and the frustrations, fears and unfulfilled feelings are still there, it is no longer acceptable for me to dismiss them.

When all that fun, superfluous and distracting stuff gets stripped away what's left is the real substance of life. The important things that truly matter. How you communicate with your partner. The relationship you have with your kids. The thoughts and feelings you cultivate on a daily basis. What your life looks like and how you want it to be.

This book is about what happens when you don't get what you think you want and instead get what you really need. This is your opportunity to consider how to make the most of, and commit to loving, your one and only life.

This won't happen overnight, but what could be more worthwhile?

And I must admit, the wisdom in these pages is not a panacea. Your life won't be perfect. But even a slight shift, even a one percent change, will help you tap back into your awesomeness once again.

It's not the most glamorous work but it is, without doubt, very rewarding.

. . .

Definitions

What do I mean by embrace your awesomeness? Let's get some brief definitions out of the way and then see if this book is for you. (Hint: it is.)

Awesome: traditionally, awesome means inspiring awe, great admiration, wonder or reverence. Nowadays, more informally, it means terrific, impressive, outstanding, remarkable or excellent. Any of these definitions, traditional or modern, sound great to me.

Awesomeness: the quality of being extremely good or amazingly impressive.

I firmly believe every single one of us is extremely good or amazingly impressive as a birthright. We don't have to be or do anything in particular to be awesome. We are already awesome because we are here on this planet. I don't want, for one instant, for you to think that embracing your awesomeness means you have to change yourself into someone else.

Embrace your awesomeness means clearing away the culturally conditioned clutter, the learned negative thought patterns and the shame of somehow not living up to some lofty idea, and simply being the best person you were born to be. It is becoming untethered from societal norms that keep you small. It is not about fixing you as you are not broken.

It is about becoming the real you.

Being awesome, in the context of this book, means accepting and loving yourself just as you are PLUS accepting that you are here to reach your potential. You can love your body and want to lose weight. You can enjoy your job and want to become the vice president of the company. You can feel content in your marriage and want to be swept off your feet on a romantic date night.

These two concepts may rub up against one another, they may seem like a paradox, but you can accept them both. Think of them as the flip sides of the same coin. Life loves presenting us with paradoxes and receiving them with grace is a helpful strategy to learn.

Ultimately, appreciating your imperfectly awesome self will allow you to grow into who you were always meant to be, reach your potential and share your gifts with the world.

I can't think of anything more meaningful to do with your life. Can you?

Who is this Book For and Not For?

Initially this book was going to be written with mamas in mind but with the global pandemic going on, it was just too important to narrow down its focus. This book is for anyone, 9 to 90, who is struggling. You are not sure what day it is, let alone how you are supposed to make the best of it.

Who is this book not for?

- Someone who is truly happy and content with their life
- Negative or pessimistic people who are not prepared to change

Read this book if—like me—you:

- Feel like you are lost in the day-to-day
- Can't just settle for a mundane life on autopilot
- Have a repetitive, persistent thought of 'Is this it?'

- Know there must be more to life than how you are living it
- Don't know who you are anymore (or perhaps never knew)
- Want to NOT feel tired, overwhelmed, stressed out and stuck
- Have a hunger inside of you, a longing for more meaning in your life
- Want to reconnect with the core you that whispers to you now and then
- Are up for a challenge and willing to experiment a little with your life to bring back your awesomeness

Please note that if you are going through a diagnosed medical issue, chronic sickness, a life upheaval or a tragedy, there are more suitable books and resources out there to support you, although the tips in here can help as well. And if you suspect your issues may be coming from a more serious cause—perhaps an undiagnosed mental or physical illness—I don't want to diminish the seriousness of your situation. Please seek appropriate professional advice.

Still here? Great!

Let's get this party started.

Passwords and Ice

A couple of years ago, the expert who was tasked with prescribing the best practice for computer passwords stated that most of his advice was completely wrong. You shouldn't change your password every 90 days or use strings of meaningless letters, numbers and symbols. This just frustrates users and can be easier to hack! The current advice is to not change your password unless you believe there has been a security breach and to use a string of correctly-spelled words instead of a nonsensical jumble.

What do you do with a very sore muscle or strain? Put ice on it? Recently, a meta-analysis of scientific papers in the area of athletic injuries stated there was insufficient evidence to suggest that ice helps. The doctor who first promoted ice along with rest, compression and elevation ('RICE') even says ice may delay healing. Either rest or move the injured part of your body as you see fit, but never, ever ice it.

I was in my late thirties before I found out that there is a small arrow next to the fuel gauge in my car that tells me what side the fuel tank is on, how to properly open a Oxo cube packet, and that there is only supposed to be one space after a period, not two.

The following is attributed to Mark Twain, but, ironically, I am not sure if he actually said it: "What gets us into trouble is not what we don't know. It's what we know for sure that just ain't so."

These stories illustrate that no one really knows what they are doing, even so-called experts. Nobody has it all figured out. When you think about it, this is life. How on earth would we know what to do for our entire lives in every circumstance? We learn and grow by trying, seeing what fails and what works and doing more of the latter. All of life is built on people who are not sure but prepared to take action regardless of the outcome. This is what makes life interesting.

Our deep need for safety, certainty and predictability is discussed in the next chapter, but know for now that your quest for the 'truth' is perfectly normal AND it is not really helping you. Approaching life like a fun game or rough experiment is not easy, but it is beneficial in the long run.

Embrace Your Awesomeness

If you get nothing else out of this book, then instead of asking, 'Is this true?', ask 'Is this helpful?'

I get it, you may not want to adopt these ideas just yet. They are planted here as seeds and the book will grow them out further. For now, remember this story as told by the late educator and speaker, Sir Ken Robinson, in one of his fantastic TED talks. Once upon a time, there was a music teacher in Liverpool in the mid-twentieth century who had two of the Beatles, George Harrison and Paul McCartney, in his class. He didn't think either of them had any real musical talent or potential as musicians.

Why Me?

I was extremely reluctant to write this book as I certainly don't have it all figured out, but then I thought about all these stories and realized I had to. The only question to answer is, would the book be helpful? And of course, even if the only person it helps is me, the answer is yes.

I hope some readers come along for the ride. But even if I am the only one who relearns how to navigate life's paradoxes including how to enjoy the day-to-day while also trying to reach my potential, this book is worth my time and effort.

Writing the book, in itself, is the embodiment of embracing my own awesomeness. I can't tell you to be vulnerable, step out of your comfort zone and show your creative side if I am not willing to do it. I need to walk the walk too.

Why me? Why NOT me?

While we are on a roll of quotes that may or may not have the right attribution, as Gandhi perhaps said: "Be the change you want to see in the world."

Why Now?

This pandemic is your invitation to embrace your awesomeness —find the real you and tap into your full potential. The whole world is banana-pants crazy. Nothing is 'right' anymore. What we knew as 'correct' is being thrown into chaos. It is time to question everything.

Yes, no one wants to go through this, but it's a worldwide wake up call.

The whole world has been knocked off its axis so it's the perfect time to take a good hard look at your life. Don't wait any longer. The world will never be the same again, so why should you? This is a global reset, unprecedented in our lifetimes, and what it means for YOU is that you don't have to succumb to culturally conditioned, and mostly detrimental, norms any more.

Nothing is the norm. Isn't that great?

This book will help you unlearn these socially-ingrained beliefs, take your life off autopilot, be present and remember your true nature. On a deeper level, we already know these are crucial aspects to a life well-lived. How to tap into them is not new, it is a relearning that brings ourselves back home, brings our awesomeness back.

If you are reading this book way into the future when this pandemic is consigned to the history books, I can guarantee that there will still be something banana-pants crazy going on in the world or in your personal life that means this book is helpful and relevant. Holocaust survivor and author, Viktor Frankl, wrote in *Man's Search for Meaning*, many years ago, "For the world is in a bad state, but everything will become still worse unless each of us does his best." Pandemic or not, the wisdom in these pages is evergreen.

We can't hide anymore. We need to play the hand we have been dealt. We have to learn to live with each other. And we really need to be kinder to ourselves.

It is never the right time so what are you waiting for?

Think of this book as your permission slip to shine.

Maximum Uncertainty

More than anything, the pandemic has brought about a lot of uncertainty. We don't know how long it will last. We are not sure what it means for the economy, the environment and the general health of the world. While I'm writing this, it's not known if a vaccine will be developed, whether it will work and how it could be rolled out to billions of people.

If there is anything we DO know, it's that none of us likes feeling out of control. At least you have one tool to help with that: asking whether something is helpful. More tools will be presented in the awesomeness makeover later. It's time now to understand why we dislike feeling unstable. The exact reasons are discussed in the next chapter.

3
THE LIZARD AND OUR NEED FOR CERTAINTY

 'You may not control all the events that happen to you, but you can decide not to be reduced by them.' – Maya Angelou

Prizegiving Embarrassment

In my last year of high school at the end-of-year prizegiving, I won an award for the most conscientious and diligent student. Basically, it was a consolation prize. I wasn't the top student, but I had fairly decent grades because, boy, did I work hard. I spent every spare moment studying, forsaking hobbies, family and even hanging with my friends.

At the time, I told myself I worked hard because I needed a high grade on my exams to get onto a particular university degree path. Now, I look back and see that a primary driver of studying so much was my powerful need for certainty. Studying and getting good grades gave me control over one of the only areas of my life I knew I was good at: being a great (conscientious and diligent) student.

I didn't just work hard; I worked hard to try and figure out the world. My statistics project was on winning the lottery. I was trying to find statistically significant incidences of certain numbers being pulled out. I was constantly trying to find order in complete randomness.

I couldn't control my family life—my parents had divorced a few years previously and my father was recently remarried. I didn't know what my future held—after 12 years in the school system, I was about to be thrown out into the big wide world. And it wasn't like I had been focused on much extracurricular activity—I didn't participate in sports and had no real hobbies, so I always felt like a novice, and therefore, had insecurities in those areas.

As I started to walk onto the stage to collect my prize, my mother stood up. She was sitting in middle of the full school hall with the other parents. Overcome with pride for her eldest daughter, she cry-shouted, booming over the polite applause, "That's my big girl!" Every single student, teacher and parent (it seemed at the time), turned and stared at my mother. There was a brief silence, then some laughter and finally, after what seemed like a glacial pause, a settling down with more clapping as I collected my award and scurried off the stage.

I was absolutely mortified. It was the most embarrassing moment of my teenage years. Striving for certainty over my school work led to one of the most out-of-control situations of my young life.

Now, as a mama myself, I completely understand my mother's unfiltered reaction. It is endearing just how delighted she was in her "big girl." However, it just goes to show that the universe has funny ways of throwing you into the deep end of the uncertainty pool when you are trying not to get wet at all.

The Lizard

We have a lizard that resides in our brains. We are evolutionarily hardwired for survival. In prehistoric times, we needed a robust flight, fight or freeze mechanism for when we spotted a sabertoothed tiger, or when it spotted us. In our heads is a little area near the brain stem called the amygdala, and it prompts us to constantly scan for anything that can kill us.

In caveperson times, anything that could kill us was usually either **scary**—large beasts with sharp teeth, or **scarce**—lack of food, water or shelter. As this is a survival tool from a primitive era, the author, coach, and wise soul, Martha Beck, describes this part of us as 'The Lizard'. Others have called it the chatterbox (Susan Jeffers), the obnoxious roommate (Arianna Huffington), or —excuse the potty mouth—the 'bee-arrcch' (me).

Let's stick with Martha Beck's description for now. The Lizard is a reptilian animal in your brain that perks its head up and alerts you to anything you perceive as scary or scarce. It does this to protect you, but it means your brain is wired to find the negative at all times. It tells you nasty stuff and is generally responsible for all your damaging thoughts, especially critical self-talk.

There are two main points here. First, you must start to think of it, whatever it is, as a separate thing. It is not 'you'. It is a tiny part of your brain pelting you with fearful thoughts and feelings. I repeat, it is not YOU. I like the idea of a lizard since I can picture it in my head.

The second main point to pick up is that The Lizard tells you things are scary or scarce even if in reality they are neither. It alters your perception. Despite the current global pandemic going on as I write this, you, in the western world, live in one of the most abundant and safe times in human history. As there is nothing really dangerous going on and you have enough to eat, The Lizard turns its attention to other things it thinks you might like to worry about.

The Lizard now tells you day in and day out that you lack time, energy, money or love. Think about that for a moment, instead of being scarce in water, food, shelter and warmth, your Lizard brain is trying to protect you by telling you that time, energy, money or love are scarce and need to be conserved. It is fake fear, but it feels very real.

You rush around like you are escaping from a predator, active and alert, but most of the rush is to escape your own worries.

You get an email from your boss saying that he wants you in a meeting in thirty minutes about that project you just handed in. What does The Lizard say to you? That you must have done a great job and he wants to give you a raise? Doubtful. The Lizard tells you that the project was not up to standard, your reputation is ruined and you are about to be fired. You get a call from school saying your eldest started a playground scuffle. What do you think first? Is he a bully? I am a terrible mother? He will now never get into college? Your partner comes home from work and turns the TV on without much of a greeting. Is he angry with you for something or is he simply exhausted? The Lizard likes to make everything personal, even if someone else's behavior has nothing to do with you. It does this to protect you, but in doing so it fills you with negative and fearful thoughts.

The good news is that you can override The Lizard, your primitive alarm system. First name it. Yes, name it. I named mine Penelope and she is a real bee-arrcch. She tells me all sorts of crappy thoughts and wakes me up at 3am to bombard me with them. SHE, Penelope Lizard, is not ME, and so I don't have to take her seriously. When Penelope wakes me up, I tell her that she is being silly. I shush her and tell her to go back to sleep. Works like a charm. But I am getting ahead of myself. This is not a solutions chapter. Let's continue.

The Need for Certainty

The Lizard, more than anything, craves certainty at all times. It thinks our lives depend on it, so order and predictability are prioritized over everything else. As a survival mechanism, this has kept humanity from being wiped out for thousands of years. It is designed to protect us, and it does a great job of that.

Certainty in itself is not all bad. After all, it is a need for certainty, to try and figure things out, that has driven me to write this very book! My inner study nerd, hard at work, again. Of course, it's important to have controls around how much money you spend, have a routine bedtime and not allow your kids ice cream for breakfast every morning. Having a daily schedule, putting limits on your screen time and attempting some exercise regularly are all modern ways that certainty makes life easier. We need to believe that the cars on the other side of the road will stay there.

But this underlying need for security, although helpful to a degree, can be harmful. In this contemporary world, all that focus on certainty—safety, security, control, predictability and comfort—can come at a great cost.

There are many ways certainty can be damaging. Let's focus on three big impacts in this chapter.

Certainty versus Your Body

Just the impact on your body alone could fill a thesis. Let's check in on how you are. Right now, unclench your jaw, drop your shoulders and relax your tongue. Were these parts tense? How is this helpful?

Craving certainty drives us to blindly adhere to rules and conventions rather than listen to the inherent, but awfully quiet, wisdom of our bodies. We learn to finish everything on our plate rather than stop eating when we feel full. We let our negative thoughts and outside influences override our intuition. And we binge-watch the latest must-see late into the night rather than trudge off to bed.

Our tight need for control keeps not only our behaviors, but our bodies firmly rigid. This is obviously not good for us.

Certainty versus Variety

The universe is quite crafty, so along with certainty, we all also have a strong need for variety. This is the paradox of happiness. As discussed, the universe loves a good paradox. But novelty can take a back seat when certainty drives our lives.

In my mid-twenties, a kind but firm friend dragged me along to dance class. I hadn't taken any dance lessons in my entire life. The Lizard was telling me that I would never pick up the steps, was likely to trip up and basically look stupid the whole time. Instead, I noticed that almost everyone else was new to this type of dance and after a few stumbling lessons, I started to enjoy myself. I never got to competition level, but I can still pull out a few Ceroc moves on the dance floor when the opportunity arises. I wouldn't have this confidence if I hadn't literally taken that first step.

How often have you decided not to try that new activity, travel somewhere different or start a conversation with a stranger at a party because it seemed too scary?

Certainty versus Happiness

When I wrote *Crappy to Happy*, the central theme was that being happier is harder than not being happy. As I explained in that book, this is due to our prehistoric survival instincts - yes, The Lizard. Humans are good at building brain structure from negative experiences but poor at doing the same with positive ones.

Now I think there is even more to it. Our need for certainty costs us a great deal of happiness. Not just because we won't try new things but because it constantly directs us back to our emotional home, the emotional state in which we feel most comfortable. You would think that everyone would prefer to have a content and happy emotional home, but that is not the case. As researcher, author and TED talk speaker, Brené Brown, states, when we lose our tolerance for discomfort, we lose our capacity for joy.

We find our way back to our less-than-stellar emotional home all the time. We complain to our friends endlessly about our partners instead of having the much-needed direct conversation that resolves the issue. We stay in a monotonous job as boredom is often a preferential emotion to ambition with a chance of failure. It helps answer why people vote for the party they 'always vote for' despite disagreeing with its current policies. Especially under times of stress, scurrying back to our emotional home makes us feel safe. How else do you explain why we worry so much?

In some twisted way, holding onto our worries makes us feel in control.

As author and therapist, Harriet Lerner discusses in *Why Won't You Apologize*, sometimes it is easier and more comforting to hold onto old resentments. You may not want to show you are doing okay as showing how hurt you still are proves just how badly you were treated. Anger can protect you from feeling where the real hurt lies including the responsibility you may have in it. Plus, it can keep alive the fantasy of justice with the wrong doing you have suffered.

Knowing that 'death and taxes', are the only two things we can rely on is strangely comforting. No wonder one of the top five regrets of the dying outlined by nurse and author, Bronnie Ware, is "I wish I had let myself be happier."

Tip the Scales

What do we do about this? It's all about tipping the scales in our favor so we get more of the right kind of control plus way more variety and happiness despite the inherent vulnerability and uncertainty that is associated with these lofty concepts. Exactly how we can do this is covered later in the awesomeness makeover chapters.

You may be annoyed at yourself, but remember that this chapter is simply about awareness. Don't judge your past self. Not only do you have The Lizard and its frenzied need for certainty to deal with, but also some built-in fears.

4
THE TWO PRIMARY FEARS

 'The most common way people give up their power is by thinking they don't have any.' – Alice Walker

SELF-HELP DANCE PARTY

A few years ago, I was fortunate to attend author, coach and personal development expert, Tony Robbins' signature event, Unleash the Power Within (UPW) in Sydney, Australia. If you haven't attended, it's unlike any other conference you have ever been to.

Despite the four days being long—it was the norm to return to the hotel after midnight—it was not boring for a single second. When we were not dancing to the booming music, we were frequently instructed to high five and hug fellow attendees. Every hour or two, long lines of strangers massaged each other's shoulders. There was even an opportunity to participate in a fire walk. In a nutshell, UPW was designed to make attendees feel relentless uncertainty and still feel good about it.

UPW may have a reputation as a kind of self-help dance party but it also profoundly conveyed a number of life lessons including the concept of 'The Six Human Needs'. As discussed, we have a need for **certainty**—to feel safe and secure and to know that our expectations will be met. In apparent opposition to this, we have a need for **variety**—to have surprises and spontaneity in our lives. We also have a need for **significance**—to feel important and that our lives have meaning. On the other side of the coin, we have a need for **love and connection**. The other two needs are for **growth** and **contribution**. This is an extremely concise description, and I encourage you to look up these needs in more detail. There are some great videos on YouTube on this topic. How you try and meet these needs—in positive, negative or neutral ways—plus which needs you emphasize, have a major impact on your life.

After learning about these needs and determining which ones were most predominant, a survey was done across the large crowd. If they were being honest, approximately 80% of the 5,000 attendees had the need for certainty at the top of their needs list. And of the thousands of us who had placed certainty at the top, *every single one of us* desperately wanted certainty to be not as important as the need for love and connection.

Certainty and the Two Primary Fears

Certainty helps us survive, but as we can see with the examples around it reducing variety and happiness, it doesn't allow us to thrive. No illustration of this is more apparent than in its impact on relationships. There is a reason why psychologist, Abraham Maslow, put the need for safety before the need for love in his influential hierarchy.

Think about it, have you found fault or blamed your partner, even though in showing you were 'right', the relationship was damaged? Why do you reply to just one more email to get your inbox in order when your child is waiting for you to play? It is almost a cliché to think of the executive who stays late at work (something he or she can control) to escape a tumultuous home life. It is worth noting that one of the other top five regrets of the dying was, "I wish I hadn't worked so hard."

Why is it that our connection with loved ones is jeopardized so much when certainty is involved?

What The Lizard —which is supposed to be there to protect us— constantly tells us boils down to two primary fears. We fear that:

1. we are not enough and (as a result)
2. we won't be loved.

These fears are learned in childhood and reinforced over our lifetimes by our family relationships (even the most loving ones are not perfect), school, work and society in general. In Tara Brach's book, *Radical Acceptance*, she describes the Dalai Lama not understanding what the concept of 'self-hatred' was when asked about it by a meditation teacher. Maybe if you grow up in extraordinary circumstances these fears are not formed, but almost everyone has them.

This chapter aims to get a better awareness and understanding of these two primary fears. The second half of the book will provide wisdom and tools to unravel, counter or minimize them.

THE FEAR OF NOT ENOUGH

The fear that we are 'not enough' can be hard to grasp. Not enough for what, for whom? Susan Jeffers in her classic self-help book, *Feel the Fear and Do it Anyway*, explains that the fear of 'not enough' is the fear that 'I can't handle it'. 'It' being the situation at hand.

What stops us from living a successful and fulfilling life is the 'I am not X enough' belief. Replace 'X' with your lizard brain's favorites. Common ones are not young enough, not old enough, not thin enough, not rich enough, not pretty enough, not smart enough. Next time you stop yourself from doing something that would ultimately benefit you, pause and ask yourself gently what 'not X enough' and thus, what 'I can't handle it' belief is behind it. For example, 'I am not old enough to be the team manager' could mean that you don't feel like you have the skills, experience or maturity required to take on the new role. Half the battle is figuring out exactly what The Lizard is telling you amongst all its general, negative chatter, so try to do this with as little judgement and with as much curiosity as you can muster.

We also think there is 'not X enough' externally. Not enough time, money, energy. Nothing for dinner. Little opportunity to play with the kids. Always tired. Marketers tap into our 'not enough' fear, and use phrases such as 'bargain', 'clearance sale', 'today only' and 'just 5 left' to convey scarcity when there really is none.

Activist and speaker, Lynne Twist, has the best illustration of 'not enough'. She states that for many of us, our first waking thought of the day is 'I didn't get enough sleep' and the next one is 'I don't have enough time.' She then goes on to say that, "before we even sit up in bed, before our feet touch the floor, we're already inadequate, already behind, already losing, already lacking something. And by the time we go to bed at night, our minds are racing with a litany of what we didn't get, or didn't get done, that day."

In *Daring Greatly*, Brené Brown says that the opposite of scarcity, which The Lizard is trying to protect you from, is not abundance. It is simply 'enough'.

Your lizard brain is trying to help you but it is preventing you from accepting your true self.

THE FEAR OF NOT BEING LOVED

As babies we need connection and attachment to survive our first few years. We associate staying alive with needing love. An unfortunate side effect of The Lizard's job is that it creates a fear-based belief that we won't be loved. As adults we don't need love to survive (although it's preferred). However, thanks to The Lizard we think we are scarce in the one thing we have the greatest fear of losing.

Thus, we scramble to get what we think is love and connection in any form that is offered, even if it is doing more to hurt us. This goes a long way to explaining why women and men stay in violent relationships but it also helps us understand other detrimental behaviors like people pleasing and playing small (more on these in the next chapter).

In other words, we strive for love because The Lizard creates fake fear that tells us that our lives depend on getting love. Instead, we often only get comfort (certainty) as the last thing we want to do is to expose our vulnerability. These are powerful concepts and they are hard to accept, but please don't dismiss them.

Believe me, I also don't want to think of myself as an anxious person driven by The Lizard who seeks out love at any cost, but some of my behavior conveys this so perfectly there is an obvious truth to it. When, late in the evening, I stand in my dark kitchen bathed in the light of the refrigerator, I have to own up to the fact that the sweet thing I am craving is probably not contained inside it.

Jennifer Pastiloff writes in her wonderful memoir, *On Being Human*, that she thought for certain that loving someone fully would kill her, that it would cause her body to rupture. Maybe not everyone feels quite that strongly but if love is associated with losing yourself, figuratively or literally, no wonder we prefer certainty.

The Equation

The bottom line of The Lizard + Certainty + Primary Fears equation is low self-love. Remember, this whole equation is not YOU, just a culturally constructed problem that you can dismantle. Removing parts of this equation means getting back in touch with who you really are, loving yourself no matter what and living a life of freedom and joy.

It means embracing your awesomeness.

First, we need to get clear on what self-love is and distinguish it from similar concepts. Here come the definitions.

Definitions

Self-love: appreciation, regard or belief for your own worth, value, happiness and wellbeing

Self-worth: a sense of one's own value or worth as a human, or, as described by Adia Gooden in her TEDx talk, 'Cultivating Unconditional Self-Worth', "the sense that you deserve to be alive, to be loved and cared for and to take up space."

Self-esteem: confidence and belief in your worth, value and abilities, often used interchangeably with self-respect

Self-confidence: trust in one's abilities, qualities and power

When I wrote *Find Your Purpose in 15 Minutes*, I found myself in a research rabbit hole. I was trying to distinguish between purpose, meaning, destiny, mission, fate and a calling. Now, I find myself with the same issue.

Do me a favor and read those definitions again.

I don't know about you, but I can't see a whole lot of difference between self-love, self-worth, self-esteem, self-confidence or self-respect.

But what does it really matter? We tend to trip up on language and stop ourselves from seeing the bigger picture. Let's spend as short amount of time as we can here and move on to the more important stuff–changing our lives for the better.

I can't tell you how much I didn't want the answer to the equation to be self-love. I can barely say the word 'self-love'. It sounds a little sketchy to me, perhaps alluding to a more, shall we say, *intimate*, meaning. And it's sometimes associated with vanity or narcissism.

Right up until I wrote this section, I was using self-worth or self-esteem as stand-ins. But I don't want to shy away from the real issue and the real answer. If you want, when self-love is mentioned, exchange it for a more sanitized version.

I no longer want to downplay self-love.

We all need to relearn how to cultivate unconditional self-love. You need to, as Kamal Ravikant says in his book of the same name, love yourself like your life depends on it.

A Perfect Storm

Between The Lizard, your desperate need for certainty, the primary fears that you are not enough and won't be loved, and your extreme vulnerability, it is amazing that you are even able to get out of bed in the morning and function at all! You have a perfect storm of crappiness!

Please raise one hand above your head and bend it at the elbow so your hand rests on the back of your shoulder. Give yourself a pat on the back. Congratulations, not only do you get out of bed every morning, but you are trying grow and love the awesome human you were born to be. You are to be commended.

You have also gotten through this chapter, and this is a very hard chapter! Now that you know all this stuff, there is no going back. You have woken up. The first step is awareness, which you have conquered. Your brain is a tool that you want working for you, not against you. Your thoughts, emotions and hence behaviors and habits are all within your control. Isn't this a great notion? You strive for certainty and it has been within you all along.

Before we get to how you can usher yourself into awesomeness, it is important to see exactly how this lack of self-love has a harmful impact on your life. It's time to check in with The Four Hazards: perfectionism, procrastination, people pleasing and playing small.

5
THE FOUR HAZARDS

 'Never put off until tomorrow what you can do the day after tomorrow.' – Mark Twain

MUTANT ORANGE CATERPILLARS

My friend told me this story of a time she found some monarch caterpillars in her backyard that had no food as they had eaten all the leaves of the swan plant they were on. A neighbor said he heard that feeding caterpillars pumpkin was a good substitute for the nourishment they usually get from a swan plant. This was in the days before the Internet when it was harder to check these things.

As she wanted to help out the caterpillars, my friend cut up bits of pumpkin and left it at the bottom of the stripped-bare swan plant. After a couple of weeks, she discovered that the caterpillars had morphed from their usual black, white and yellow stripes into a bright, mutant orange.

More days passed. The fat, orange caterpillars managed to create hanging chrysalises from the bare branches of the swan plant. Instead of a shiny, jade color, the cocoons looked like mini ginger blimps. Only a handful of caterpillars hatched into butterflies and the ones that did couldn't open up their wings. It was a caterpillar zombie apocalypse. My friend had the best of the intentions, but unfortunately feeding the caterpillars pumpkin, although they liked it, ultimately ended them.

Our lizard brains feed us negative thought patterns to try and keep us safe. We think these help us but they stop us from living a truly fulfilling life. We grow wonky or don't grow at all. We don't transform. And we never learn to fly.

A Diagram That Will Change Your Life

Please pay attention and study the simple diagram below as it will change your life. I am not saying these words lightly. This simple arrangement of words has the potential to have a powerful impact on the rest of your life.

Are you ready? Here goes...

SITUATION / CIRCUMSTANCE ->

THOUGHT / MEANING / BELIEF ->

EMOTION / FEELING ->

ACTION / BEHAVIOR ->

OUTCOME

Your life is determined by the meanings you place on external events. Meanings you have decided upon. You decide the meaning. You.

The main thing to realize is that you have the power to control all the components in this diagram between situation and outcome. You often do not have the power over the situation or the outcome, but you can decide on the thoughts, emotions and actions in between. You wanted certainty, and it is right here for the taking. Because you have the control, you have the ability to also change your beliefs, choose your feelings and determine your behavior.

Once you understand that you are in control of your thoughts and beliefs, once you really get it, you will grasp just how powerful this concept is. Even believing that you have control over your thoughts is a belief in itself. Perhaps it is not 'the truth' but isn't it more empowering—i.e.: helpful—than the belief that you are simply a rag doll reacting to your environment?

In my book, *Crappy to Happy*, it was advised to pluck out a detrimental thought or belief and go about creating a different meaning around it. However, there are thousands of negative thoughts, so where do you start?

THE FOUR HAZARDS

This chapter identifies four common types of negative beliefs that keep us from living our best lives. These are The Four Hazards: perfectionism, procrastination, people pleasing and playing small. A hazard, as defined in health and safety literature, is 'a potential source of harm or adverse health effect on a person or persons.' These four hazardous beliefs have been selected as they are the most habitual yet highly destructive to our lives.

Health and safety best practice is to identify and manage the hazard. This means finding solutions that isolate and assess the hazard. Then it is about working to eliminate it or minimize it.

In this book, each hazard will be defined. Why we believe and take action on these hazardous patterns of living will be explained. There will be examples showing exactly why they hurt us. A couple of tools to help us all move past each of these hazards will be introduced.

The Four Hazards interrelate and feed off each other. Perfectionism, for example, can lead to procrastination. They are separated out here to make them easier to identify. You can then see which of the hazards you most relate to and where you want to direct your focus, at least at first.

Perfectionism

Perfectionism is striving for flawlessness accompanied by critical self-talk and worry about others' evaluations. A lot of perfectionism is wrapped up in what it is not. It is not seeking excellence, trying to attain success or wanting to master something. These reflect self-love. Instead, perfectionism is a fear-based response that if you could just control the outside world, everything would be all right internally. Jennifer Pastiloff, describing her serious eating disorder in her memoir, says that she thought if she could perfect her outside, no one would see how bad she believed herself to be on the inside.

At my first job out of university I was constantly staying late to get everything right. My manager told me that it was fine to go the extra mile but I didn't have to run a marathon. Perfectionism is trying to get to that elusive finish line because you think then you will finally be good enough.

The Lizard leads you to believe that perfectionism provides safety and protection but instead it presents you with a myriad of negative effects. Can you identify with these? I sure can!

Perfectionism:

- Keeps you busy as that 'proves' you have value
- Means being hard on yourself and overly critical when things go wrong
- Leads to never starting unless you think you can achieve 100% success
- Causes procrastination on decisions because you want them to be 'right'
- Results in difficulty saying sorry as you can't view your errors and limitations as separate from your self-worth
- Makes you think you are the only person who can do the job right so you do more than you really need and then feel exhausted
- Produces a lot of frustration, shame and anxiety even though 'perfect' people shouldn't have these emotions (perfectionists use the word 'should' a lot)

As you can see, perfectionism doesn't protect you. It does the opposite. It keeps you small, stressed and stuck. It tries to fix your lack of self-love. What happens instead, when you inevitably fall short, is a reinforcement of your unworthiness, of not being good enough.

If you want to break the perfectionist cycle of doom, you don't have to race through to the later chapters. Here a two mini-tools that will help you right now.

1. UTILIZE BLACK AND WHITE THINKING

Perfectionism is associated with black and white thinking, and this can be twisted to your advantage. Instead of striving for a perfect 10 on a range of poor to perfect, instead decide that 'perfect' means done as opposed to not done. Two choices. Not a range. Is something done? Good, check it off.

2. Chunk Down and Celebrate

Break down big challenges into bits of progress, then celebrate small wins along the way. Chunked progress toward a defined outcome is always preferential to staying late or remaining stuck.

Procrastination

I spent hours and hours collating songs for the various playlists for my wedding day. I doubt anyone even heard the 'dinner' playlist. Half the dance songs didn't get played because the speeches ran too long. I am not sure if anyone would even remember my hand-picked song that I walked down the aisle to. All that time creating wedding song playlists and not once did I do any planning for married life.

Procrastination is simple to understand, extremely common and very easy to do. In short, it is delaying, postponing or avoiding a task that needs to be done. That's all. The more interesting question is, why do we procrastinate?

The main cause of procrastination is that the completed task occurs in the future. We have to take action to attain the good feelings associated with finishing it. But the lizard brain likes comfort so we are all pleasure-seeking machines. We want to feel good now. Watching TV is more enjoyable than tidying up the house, even if you add a little guilt or stress on the side.

Unfortunately, feeling good now reinforces our feelings of not being good enough if there are more important things to do. I should know. Instead of outlining this very book—a guide that is concerned with solving the problem of procrastination—I spent over an hour watching a Beatles tribute concert!

Procrastination is insidious and can manifest in the following ways:

- Being busy
- Being distracted
- Doing the less urgent, smaller or more pleasurable tasks first
- Focusing on other 'shiny objects' rather than the important task at hand

The trouble is that all the ways that procrastinating occurs can also be justified. Perhaps you really are too busy at work to train for that marathon. Maybe you need a break and a bit of mindless scrolling helps you to relax. Often, I find that checking off a few emails and rearranging my to-do list gets me in the right head space to start writing. Occasionally, you may work out that the thing that has been sitting forever on your to-do list may not be anything you need to do. I thought I should create a podcast and when I simply removed it from my to-do list, I felt immense relief.

Try not to judge, but with a childlike curiosity ask yourself why you're not taking action on what you are supposed to be doing. Are you trying to avoid the boredom of the task? Are you attempting to numb the fear of failure? Is keeping busy a way to not do the most crucial things? These may hit home but getting honest with yourself about why procrastination keeps happening goes a long way to minimizing this hazard.

Here are two interrelated suggestions to help you boot procrastination to the curb:

. . .

1. **ASSOCIATE GOOD FEELINGS WITH TAKING ACTION**

Place more value on the emotions you get from taking action than from procrastinating. Decide that feeling accomplished is more important than short-term pleasure. Add a ton more positive feelings into the task by making it simpler to begin with or dividing it into smaller parts, then revel in milestones.

2. **ASSOCIATE BAD FEELINGS WITH NOT TAKING ACTION**

Allow yourself to feel the guilt, stress, overwhelm and anxiety from not doing or delaying an important task. Often, we only think of the future boredom or fear, but letting in the negative emotions related to procrastinating, although not fun, is integral with living up to your expectations.

PEOPLE PLEASING

People pleasing comes from our inherent need for approval, attention and affection. This is not bad in itself. As discussed, we need these to form attachments to survive as babies. The issue with people pleasing arises when we use it to continually help us feel in control, to feel like we are enough and to feel loved.

Why do we do it? Here are three reasons:

- It feels wonderful to be appreciated (I love every single five-star book review)
- We believe it minimizes criticism and rejection (unfortunately though the one-star reviews still happen)
- And this is the big one – it means that if we are running around constantly trying to please others, we don't have to deal with our own lives (ouch!)

Wrapping your self-worth into your need for approval doesn't serve you.

Here are the main negative outcomes of being a people pleaser:

- It makes you feel like you can't handle criticism or rejection
- You don't say 'no' and end up feeling resentful and exhausted
- Self-esteem bound to outside sources makes you feel less in control
- You never get what you really want as you are too afraid to speak up
- It suffocates your dreams as you try not to stand out or go for your goals
- Justifies putting relationships above your own self, like 'they' matter more
- It keeps you thinking you must be nice because you don't want to be seen as bossy, selfish, uptight or arrogant

Obviously, you need to separate your innate self-worth—knowing that you are enough and lovable just as you are—from your need for approval. It's imperative for you to be yourself. As author and therapist, Edith Eger states, "when we come to believe that there is no way to be loved and to be genuine, we are at risk of denying our true nature." Remember, you are not chocolate—not everyone has to like you.

What is interesting is that people pleasing often doesn't help the people you are trying to please. You aren't a sociopath, you do want to give to others. But there is a line where this doesn't serve you or them. If you are feeling overworked, taken advantage of and have no time for yourself, then you can bet you are not letting others take control of their own responsibilities, growth and emotions. You may even be robbing them of the vital need to help, serve or give to you.

This is true for couple relationships, in the workplace and with family and friends. And this is especially relevant for parents—of course we want our kids to be happy and have a contented life. Brené Brown says that the bravest thing we can do is let our kids struggle and experience adversity. No one said parenting was easy! This does not mean throwing them in the deep end of the pool but it does mean keeping up the swim lessons even if they don't feel like it that day.

We've established people pleasing is not good for you OR the people you want to please. Here are two ways to limit your need for approval:

1. Understand the Two Types of People

I believe there are two types of people. Those who will like you regardless and those who won't like you no matter what you do. Only listen to and hang out with the first type.

2. Say No

I've written about it in my other books but it is worth repeating here. Just say 'no'. Say 'no' nicely. Say 'no' directly. Say 'no' with humor. Say it however you can and wherever you can. Practice it. Make it a habit. 'No' really is a complete sentence. It's just so incredibly important that there will be more tips on saying 'no' later.

Playing Small

Embrace Your Awesomeness

When I came back from working odd jobs and traveling overseas in my mid-twenties, I decided to retrain as an accountant. (Side note: isn't it interesting that I wanted to have a 'secure' career after so much out-of-comfort-zone activity?). I worked out I needed to study accounting for one year to get the qualification I needed. I was joining students who were in their fourth year of university. Two months after I started, all the large accounting firms initiated their recruitment for graduates for the following year. These were the best jobs available for accounting students fresh out of university. Everyone else knew this was coming but it was a complete surprise to me. I soon realized that despite knowing almost no accounting, not owning any corporate clothes and having little time to prepare for interviews, I would have to apply right away.

Striving for control at any cost and allowing fear to direct your life leads you to play small. Playing small can manifest via low self-esteem, imposter syndrome, nagging self-doubt or lack of confidence. Playing small is a good catch-all phrase for these hazards because, although they are all slightly different, there is also much overlap. And, er, I like alliteration and it goes well with the other P's. At the end of the day, they are all hazardous beliefs you adopt. They are not the 'truth' about you, they are not helpful and they are certainly not who you are deep down. Tara Brach says, "It is a waste of our precious lives to carry the belief that something is wrong with us."

Let's see what each means.

Low Self-Esteem: self-esteem is the belief you are valuable; low self-esteem is feeling bad, having a low opinion or not approving or respecting yourself.

Imposter Syndrome: an unreasonable feeling of being a fraud, that you are going to be 'found out', that your abilities have been overrated, that you don't deserve your success as it is due to luck or external factors.

Nagging Self-Doubt: a lack of faith in yourself, a constant feeling of doubt or uncertainty about oneself as a person; standing in your own way.

Lack of Self-Confidence: confidence is having enough faith in what you are able to do so that you take action; lack of self-confidence is characterized by low trust in your abilities, skills or being able to cope.

Boy do we love giving ourselves horrible labels! You may resonate with one description over another. Some terms go in and out of fashion. Imposter Syndrome is currently having its time in the sun. Overall, there is so little variation between these concepts that it really doesn't serve us to spend all day here.

Like perfectionism, procrastination and people pleasing, playing small means that we don't live up to our potential, go for our dreams or show up in the best way for those around us.

In particular, playing small means:

- Not asking for help
- Avoiding reasonable risks
- Never being happy with the work you do
- Believing you are incompetent and out of your depth
- Over preparing, which is time-consuming and exhausting
- Never feeling ready or skilled enough (see the 'enough' in there?)
- Having feelings of stress and anxiety as you are sure you will be 'found out'

Embrace Your Awesomeness

You know these hazards are not serving you but the labels seem too entrenched. How do you shake them off? Here are two mini-tools:

1. Praise Yourself

Every little thing you do, give yourself a pat on the back. You want to be valued, lessen the self-doubt, not feel like an imposter? Notice all the things you do and give yourself a high five for them. It may seem ridiculous but the only way to build self-esteem back up is to approve of yourself. You are not helping the world by sitting in your own insecurities. Nourish yourself with positive feedback today.

2. Act Now

These playing small beliefs come about because you know you don't understand everything but need to act. This is a sign you are competent, not incompetent. You are enough! Imperfectly taking action is one way to forge more confidence and self-esteem. Go do that thing.

Under the guise of low self-esteem, imposter syndrome, nagging self-doubt, lack of confidence or whatever it was called, I wanted to hide away when it came to those graduate recruitment sessions. Instead, I got a friend to test me on a bunch of interview questions, borrowed a dress suit and arrived early. I ended up with four offers from four of the top accounting firms. Imperfect action wins out over playing small every time.

The Good News

This may seem like a lot to take on! Different areas of your life may highlight your people pleasing behaviors, or you may remember times when you played small. Perfectionism or procrastination or a combination of both may resonate deeply with you.

The Four Hazards are prevalent, common and detrimental but the good news is they can be eliminated or minimized. Remember, they are merely negative beliefs and bad habits. They are coping mechanisms you grab onto to help you stay above the water despite almost drowning in your need for certainty and your lizard brain fears.

They are not you.

In the second half of this book are the four solutions and their associated tools of awesomeness that will clear away these hazards. What is left after the declutter is a simple life of freedom and joy.

Ready to get started?

6
AWESOMENESS MAKEOVER

 'If you are always trying to be normal, you will never know how amazing you can be.' – Maya Angelou

TOP OF THE WORLD

Can you recall your first childhood memory? How old were you? What were you doing? I have a vague recollection of going down the slide on my first day of kindergarten when I was three years old. This stands out in my memory because that slide was wide—big enough for two kids side-by-side at once—but I didn't realize this when I started sliding down it. I tried to hold onto both sides, but I couldn't, so I held onto one side and then bumped unevenly down the short slope to the bottom. It didn't really hurt but it wasn't the whooshing glide I had envisaged it would be. I felt disappointed, a bit embarrassed and a little sore. It took the encouragement of a kind teacher to get me to play on the slide again.

At an event I went to a couple of years back we did an exercise that expanded our first childhood memory. We were instructed to go back a few moments before the actual memory began. I instantly knew what happened beforehand. I was at the top of the slide looking down, nothing in my mind except the anticipation of joy. I was on top of the world! The little girl at the bottom of the slide was the same little girl who was at the top except she had learned fear and taken on uncertainty. I know deep down I still have that little girl at the top of the world inside of me. I need to reconnect with her again.

Awesomeness Makeover

This is an 'awesomeness makeover' as it is not about changing who you really are. It's an unlearning in which you start to peel away all that negative cultural conditioning and constant lizard brain fears. Your foundation is solid, but a lick of paint and a few throw cushions would liven everything up.

This book takes what the most successful and fulfilled people do and don't do and divides them into four areas. To minimize or eliminate The Four Hazards of perfectionism, procrastination, people pleasing and playing small that are currently operating in your life, there are The Four Solutions:

- Self-Love
- Security and Control
- Social Awesomeness
- Step Out of Your Comfort Zone

Each of these four solutions will take up the next four chapters but you may have some preliminary questions. Let's tackle these.

. . .

Q&A

What if I am not sure I even want to change my life?

If you are truly content and happy, then what are you doing reading this book? If you are feeling even a little bit homesick for your deeper self, long for more nourishing relationships or constantly feel overwhelmed, then you are in the right place. Why not try the awesomeness makeover and see if it is for you? If not, you can always go back to your normal life. Remember, I am not asking you to change your life as such. Instead, this book helps you clear away the garbage so you can focus on the most important things: loving yourself and others, feeling in control and reaching your true potential.

Maybe I could do with an awesomeness makeover but can this really work? I mean, isn't everything locked up in our subconscious or something like that?

You can change your thoughts, beliefs, emotions and actions at any time. There is a fun challenge at the end of this chapter that demonstrates this. Remember the 'Is it true? or, Is it helpful?' tool? Believing that change is hard or impossible is not helpful. It is true that some of these hazardous patterns are deeply ingrained but that does not mean you can't change them. Tools such as affirmations have been shown to create new neural pathways. Tapping into your body and your intuition are direct routes to your subconscious. Taking action outside of your comfort zone builds new beliefs.

I don't want to be brainwashed, is this what this is?

Er, no. It takes a conscientious effort from you to change learned behaviors. This book can provide the solutions but can't do the work for you. Anyway, what have you got against brainwashing? Some brains could do with a bit of a wash!

Does this take willpower?

If you think it takes a ton of willpower, then you won't take action. There is a provocative notion floating around at the moment that there is no such thing as willpower. Consider that for a moment. If there is actually no such thing as willpower, then what does embracing your awesomeness really involve? I believe it involves making a decision and then building a lovable self-identity and positive habits around the new choice.

Is this a panacea for all my problems?

No. But if you are even one percent happier or more fulfilled isn't it worth the trouble? This is about returning to the real you. I am not saying it will be easy but it will feel right. It won't stop you from having problems but you will start to have higher-level problems.

What if I don't have the time to devote to this?

Perhaps you feel that you are far too busy, that family or work is your priority or that you are too stressed or exhausted to contemplate yet another thing you should do at the moment. And yes, like you, I lead a big, full life, but I often slide into prioritizing things that do not contribute to any real, lasting happiness. I can find myself watching a banal sitcom, shooting off an email so I can keep my inbox down and scrolling, scrolling, scrolling. Sometimes all at the same time. We all have the same 24 hours in a day, and someone out there is swimming under a waterfall, learning how to juggle or strumming their favorite song on an acoustic guitar and you are not. Are you busy being busy without adding value into your life? Our culture celebrates busyness! It normalizes stress. Don't confuse this with living a fulfilling life. Please stop lying to yourself that you are too busy—or too stressed from being so busy—to bring a bit of awesomeness back into your life.

OK, I concede that my life could be better, that this may just work and I am up for the challenge, but isn't it a little selfish?

What is selfish about wanting to become the best person you can be? What is selfish about wanting to learn and grow so can and share your unique skills, talents and gifts with the world? What is selfish about doing nice things for yourself so you can feel better and then treat others around you with respect and kindness? Do you know what I think is selfish? Allowing your need for certainty, fearful thinking and hazardous patterns such as procrastination and playing small to keep you miserable and stuck.

How can I really change unless I am hard on myself?

Author and coach, Tara Mohr writes in *Playing Big* that, "Where we think we need more self-discipline, we usually need more self-love." Working hard to get what you want is absolutely encouraged. Train for that marathon, run the race. But telling yourself you are not a success—you are not enough—unless you get to the finish line is not a healthy practice. We have to work out a way to live with the paradox that we can only be successful and happy if we are content with who we are AND also want to improve ourselves.

. . .

How do I make sure I am still thought of as a nice person?

Another way to word this is deciding that a little more confidence or self-esteem would be helpful but you don't want to be thought of as rude, bossy or arrogant. Well, you know you are a nice person, because, well, you are awesome. You can't stop caring what others think of you but can put firm boundaries up about whose opinions truly matter to you. And there are simple ways of showing assertiveness and asking for what you want without being impolite. See Chapter Nine for more.

What if this makes me stand out?

Let's get more candid and admit that what is stopping you is not the tactics or the how-to but your mindset. On the surface, it may seem strange to have fears attached to something that should be so desirable, but it's perfectly natural. After all, now you have to admit that something is missing from your life and you want it back. Any time you strive for more, for something you really want, there is fear attached. One way this shows up is a fear of attack. For instance, you don't want to stand out, be different or make a fool out of yourself in your quest to embrace your awesomeness. You want to be 'normal' but keeping to society's standards means a mediocre existence as you default to fear and negativity. Yes, this work means loving your weird self and being enthusiastic about life, even if others judge you.

What if I don't like the real me?

Now we are getting somewhere. Remember, deep down everyone is awesome. We've all made mistakes but that doesn't mean we are bad. You may not like things you have done in the past but there is still plenty of awesomeness left in the tank. Maybe the best part of all of us is the ability to grow and change. Hold onto that piece. Edith Eger writes in her holocaust memoir, *The Choice*, that our problem is "the belief that discomfort, mistakes, disappointment signal something about our worth." They don't. We deserve more than that. This is about loving the imperfect you. It is as simple as that.

WHAT DO I DO ABOUT ALL THESE EMOTIONS THAT ARE COMING UP for me?

You can now admit you want your awesomeness back in your life. You desire it, you crave it, you need it. But here is the main roadblock: embracing your awesomeness will require you to *feel* once again. Going on this journey means getting back in touch with your positive emotions. This is hard because anyone who seems truly happy can be considered at best, naïve and at worst, certifiable. How can anyone be happy when the world is bananapants crazy? Even more challenging: by allowing in the positive emotions, you also have to feel the so-called negative emotions—you can't feel just one type of emotion. And once you let yourself feel, you will feel everything. Everything. You will feel sad that you didn't do this sooner, angry that you missed out on the delight and wonder of life for so long and scared that once you regain your awesomeness you could lose it again. We are so used to numbing and distracting ourselves, that acute emotions—of any type—are avoided at all costs. Being in touch with your emotions puts you in a vulnerable state and this can be incredibly uncomfortable. The only thing you can do is feel your feelings. Let them pass through you and they will eventually dissipate. There is no need to be scared of them. You are enough and you can handle this.

. . .

Is it okay to ask for help?

Yes. Double yes. Now you are getting it. You must allow yourself to be vulnerable so you can become stronger. Asking for support is a courageous act. Top leaders put their hands up to ask questions. The Dalai Lama was asked something at a conference and pondered it for a full minute before saying "I don't know." This is the Dalai Lama—the spiritual guru who is expected to impart wisdom at any opportunity! Asking for help or support and saying you are not sure are brave choices as you could feel shame or judgement, internally or externally. Ultimately, they are the right, or let us say—the most helpful—choices as they remind us how to feel alive.

That sounds like a lot of work... and for what?

Well, maybe it's not. This is an unlearning, a stripping back to what truly gives you satisfaction and joy and nothing else. It doesn't have to take years of therapy or extraordinary willpower or changing who you essentially are. All it requires is a decision to learn to live with a bit of uncertainty while trusting you are heading in the right direction.

But I get it, I am asking you to dive into unknown waters, not knowing if you will encounter mermaids or sharks. As British comedian, Miranda Hart said on a recent Facebook Live: "We follow our hearts and sometimes our dreams come true and sometimes we get cracked open by suffering." Why would we take the risk?

Trust me when I say there is a bigger life to live. A life where you are not afraid of emotions because they make you feel alive. A life where you can fall into loving relationships and know you will be caught. A life where you achieve your goals because you are not afraid of failure. I promise that you can handle the journey, even if it gets a little bumpy, because it is beautiful and worth taking.

And if this isn't enough, do it for others. Be a role model to your children, friends or colleagues. We desperately need more great leaders in the world. Why can't it be you?

Tools and Challenges

Each of The Four Solutions has three Tools of Awesomeness that you can adopt into your life. They interrelate and build on each other but are separated out to make them more accessible. It's suggested to find two or three tools that resonate the most and focus on those first. Add in others as required.

There will be challenges at the end of each chapter relating to the tools introduced in it. Please, please do them. Add them into your life every day for the next 30 days. Give them a try. Only a month in your long, long life. You can do it. Reading this book is one thing but action is where the magic happens. The Tools of Awesomeness may seem off-putting at first but ultimately feel good. By giving them a go, you can decide which tools you want to keep for the long term. Please do the work!

As a starter to the main course, try this challenge. Practice twice a day for the next 30 days saying the alphabet backwards. That is all. By the end of the month, observe how much better you are at it.

Now that your questions have been answered you should be amped to jump into the first of The Four Solutions. Let's embrace a bit of self-love. But first, I must talk about bats.

7
SELF-LOVE

 'Love is the bridge between you and everything.' – Rumi

BAT IN A CAGE

When I was ten or eleven, I went to the local zoo with my family. It is fairly likely we got to watch the elephants and managed the right amount of badgering to secure a double scoop of ice cream but the whole day is really a blur of hazy childhood amusement. That is, except for one vibrant memory.

A lot of the zoo experience was spent trying to spot animals in their enclosures. Towards the end of the day, we came across a tall glass enclosure that held some type of bat. I went right up to the glass and looked towards the back of the pen expecting to see a bat or three hanging upside-down near the top. I placed my hand above my eyes to shade them and pressed my nose against the cold glass while I kept looking around the whole bat house trying to spot the elusive creatures. There was a shadowy plant growing at the front that was obscuring my whole view and I kept trying to look around it.

My sister, taking delight in my growing frustration, bounded up to me and pointed out the bat straight away. With long, black wings spread out around its tiny body, somehow it was perched on the glass right in front of my face. That wasn't a plant blocking my sightline but the actual bat right there, eye-level with me, with only a thin pane of glass separating us. I gasped and jumped back. My heart was beating so loudly you would have heard it if it weren't for my sister's pealing laughter.

Self-Love is the Answer

When the topic for this book was coming together it took me a very, very long time to come to the conclusion that self-love had to be at the core of the answer. I kept looking around it, hoping against hope it would be anything but that. No, not self-love! It was easy to turn a blind eye to accepting self-love as a key component but I couldn't do it forever. Glacially, I focused my vision and admitted that the very thing I had been searching for was staring me in the face all along.

If self-love is the answer, how do we manifest it? It's something that we are born with—babies demand it—that is conditioned away. It is not going to naturally spring back without a conscious effort.

Self-love is a practice.

Here are three tools to bring back self-love:

- Awesomeness Pep Talk
- Self-Love Affirmations

- Practice Self-Care

Awesomeness Pep Talk

You are the only you there is, the only you that there ever has been and ever will be. It is a miracle of biology, timing and whatever faith or science-backed belief you hold that you have arrived on this planet in your body at this time.

You are a beautiful, magnificent, unique, extraordinary miracle.

You don't need to do or be anything to embrace your awesomeness. It is your birthright because you are alive. You were awesome at birth and have the innate potential to become even more awesome.

In the past you have done stupid things, made mistakes, hurt people, haven't treated yourself or others kindly. You may feel guilt, shame, anger, sadness. And guess what? You are still unmistakably awesome. There is nothing wrong with you at your core being. Absolutely nothing.

There is no point compromising on who you are because you are worried what others may think. You deserve to live the most rich, full life there is for no reason at all. Showing up and being whoever you are is scary but trying to fit in by not being yourself is utterly exhausting. As Brené Brown writes, "True belonging doesn't require you to *change* who you are; it requires you to *be* who you are." Isn't it great that you don't have to prove you are enough, that you can just get on with living your life?

We are meant to be different. The things that are 'wrong' with us are the things that make us unique and special. Our diversity is humanity's greatest strength.

Embrace your quirks and be your unapologetically weird self.

Being authentic means being real. It means we stop being observers on the sidelines and start participating fully in the game of life. In *The Top Five Regrets of the Dying*, the number one regret was "I wish I had had the courage to live a life true to myself, not the life others expected of me." Practice being your authentic self every single day. Find ways to be real.

You are a vital piece of the puzzle. Don't deny the world its one chance to bask in your inherent brilliance. Be exactly who you are because why not? Make space for yourself. Find and own your place in this banana-pants crazy world.

And when you do show up and finally take off that armor, you will likely be pleasantly surprised at what strengths you have and what you are capable of. "We are not on this earth to accumulate victories or trophies but to be whittled down until what is left is who we truly are" says Arianna Huffington.

You are enough. More than that: you are a fabulously awesome big deal.

You deserve the very best simply because you are here. Playwright and activist

James Baldwin sums this up: "Our crown has already been bought and paid for. All we have to do is wear it."

Embrace your awesomeness today, and every day for the rest of your one precious life.

. . .

If you loved this **Awesomeness Pep Talk** and are thinking 'boy, I would love to have my own copy of this so I can read it often', then I have good news for you! Grab your one-page **Awesomeness Pep Talk** PDF (along with TheHappy20 PDF) by heading to **JulieSchooler.com/gift**.

SELF-LOVE AFFIRMATIONS

My friend and fellow author, Jennifer Hacker Pearson, The Mother Mentor, asked her Facebook group, 'The Tough Mothers Village', a question. The enquiry seemed innocuous enough but it was dropped like a bomb on the busy mamas in the group. She asked, "What if, just for today, you loved yourself as much as you love your children?" Well, the fallout was quick, painful and explosive. Responses such as "I couldn't do it...but am going to work on it" and "I will give it a shot... but it's not easy" were typical. I read this question and felt my stomach drop. Because the truth is, well, I don't love myself anywhere near like I love my kids. And there is something very, very wrong with that.

We know self-love is missing from our lives so how do we begin to invite it back in? How do we fall in love with ourselves all over again?

How do we set about loving ourselves no matter what?

First, understanding the benefits of loving yourself can help. Remember that certainty you have been craving? Well, loving yourself gives you more stability and control plus less drama and neediness as you are not relying on others to provide love to you. Self-love is the foundation that helps prop up all the other lofty goals and values you have. You can't dream big or create with passion or provide altruistic kindness without some self-love in your heart. Harriet Lerner says, "the capacity to take responsibility, feel empathy and remorse and offer a meaningful apology rests on how much self-love and self-respect that person has available. We don't have the power to bestow these traits on anyone but ourselves." Life just works better with self-love front and center.

Next, we must treat loving ourselves as a verb not a noun, an action we need to take. A daily practice. We can't move through life and just hope the love will come. We have to invite it back in, no RSVP required. This will feel strange and not like yourself and perhaps even a struggle, but what else could be more important? If you are sick you do everything in your power to get well—rest, take Vitamin C, keep up the fluids. We are all sick with self-loathing, or at least in a chronic state of mild dislike. We need to do anything we can to make ourselves feel better. You may not think you can love yourself now but try to starting believing in the possibility of cultivating it. Imagine, just imagine for one second if you had the fiercely-won belief of the late author and publisher Louise Hay when she said, "there is so much love in your heart that you could heal the entire planet."

And so we get to affirmations. I know, sorry, but there is no better way to start. Yes, I am talking about repeating things over and over, writing them down in a journal or staring deeply into your eyes in the bathroom mirror. They invade the mind with a conscious choice, overriding all those negative thought patterns. They create new mental grooves that you assimilate after a bit of practice.

Why not try it? I challenge you to one minute of self-love affirmations per day for 30 days. One lousy minute out of the 1,440 minutes in each day. Put on a timer. Do it after you brush your teeth at night or anchor it to another daily habit. Try a different one each day from the list below or select one that resonates and stick with that. Some of the affirmations are

Embrace Your Awesomeness

lighthearted, some cut deep. The trick is to say it with feeling, with intensity, like you are going to propose marriage to your sweetheart. Don't just say it, declare it or proclaim it. If you are doing it in the mirror, look into your eyes and get as close as you can. And have a bit of fun with it. Try a different pitch or tone. Whisper or shout. Smile. Move as you see fit. Try not to eye-roll. If you notice your wrinkles or grey hair, keep repeating the self-love affirmation anyway.

- I love me
- I love you
- I love myself
- I REALLY love me / you / myself
- I love me / you / myself no matter what
- I am powerful, loved, loving and I love it!
- May I love and accept myself just as I am
- I love and approve of myself exactly as I am
- Love is everywhere and I am loving and lovable

If these affirmations sound too serious, here are two quick, fun ways you can give yourself a boost with a quick dose of self-love.

1. When you say something negative about yourself, say the exact opposite in the most over-the-top, extravagant, quixotic compliment you can think of. Praise the proverbial out of yourself. No guilt or arrogance needs to be associated with this. Repeat it three times. For example, 'Hey you, you're an absolute fox today!', 'My goodness, I've never seen you look more stunning', 'You are a beautiful, creative, intelligent winner' or (taken from the amazing book and movie, *The Help*), 'You are kind, smart and important.'

2. Talk to yourself like you would talk to your dog (or other beloved pet or tiny child), e.g.: 'Hey, sweet girl', 'Look at that beautiful belly', 'You're so clever'. You get the picture.

Practice Self-Care

I absolutely hate bubble baths. Sitting around, never quite comfortable in water that is slowly getting both cold and dirty. I shudder at the instruction you read on every wellbeing top-ten list that advocates long baths like they are a cure-all. Don't get me started on lighting candles. Gah. Maybe it is the advice to take a bath at the first sign of stress or perhaps it's simply my reluctance to embrace self-love in all its forms, but it probably comes as no surprise that I have always cringed at the term 'self-care.'

What I didn't realize until now is that I have been encouraging self-care for a long time, throughout all my books. The entirety of *Rediscover Your Sparkle* is about self-care. I just called it 'sparkle strategies.'

The definition of self-care is simply caring for yourself. It is deliberately taking action to assist your health and wellbeing. It is giving yourself kindness, compassion and grace. There is nothing more loving than that. Self-care is self-love in action. It is as vital as the air you breathe. It provides you with feelings of more time, energy and abundance. You deserve as much self-care as you can get. Writer and activist, Audre Lorde said "caring for myself is not self-indulgence, it is self-preservation."

How to go about it?

The trouble is that self-care can take many forms. It may mean binge-watching the latest drama or switching off the screen and going to bed. It could mean going for a run or playing with the kids or snuggling up with a good book. It could mean sharing a bottle of bubbles with your friends or swearing off alcohol for a time. It could mean no sugar and it could mean indulging in that expensive box of chocolates you were given for your birthday. Self-care will look different across the days and years.

The actual form self-care takes is up to you. How do you decide? Self-care is about feeling good from the inside out, not just the Instagram-perfect outside. In order to work out what you really need, ask yourself any of these questions. The self-care form will arise from the answers:

- What would a wise person do?
- What would my future self want me to do here?
- What would I do if I were to treat myself like the precious human I am?
- From *Love Yourself Like Your Life Depends On It* - If I loved myself would I do this thing?

Here are general categories of self-care with some specific activities that help me by making me feel in control of my body, relationships and actions. Choose what you like from the list of categories and ideas or work out your own best practices.

Category and Ideas

- Move – walk, swim, dance, yoga
- Rest – meditate, take a nap, go to bed before 10 o'clock
- Stop – take a deep breath, look at the moon, smell the roses
- Give – help out friends, practice random acts of kindness, volunteer
- Heal – talk with a trusted person and do work to mend inner wounds
- Play – have fun with the kids, play games, read a book, listen to music

- Grow – read to learn, listen to podcasts and talks, watch documentaries
- Kind – smile, laugh, be grateful, say loving things to myself and others
- Write – research, write and publish blog posts, articles and books
- Nature – go out in the sun, spend time in the garden, be in nature
- Connect – talk, listen, hug, share a meal, spend quality time with people
- Excite – waterslides, rollercoasters, trying a new activity, e.g.: disc golf
- Indulge – TV, travel, shopping, beauty treatments, go to a movie or show
- Nourish – eat lots of vegetables, drink water, and take the utmost enjoyment in a delicious and nourishing variety of food

Self-care is also wrapped around the suggestions in the following chapters. Saying no, building healthy habits and scheduling in some time to create are all forms of self-care. They are not the traditionally soft and fluffy forms like a lot of those listed above, but they are just as important.

Start Over

The most important part of giving your beautiful, magnificent, unique, extraordinary self the most love and care you can possibly handle is to not beat yourself up if you fail miserably at it! I have to admit I started mirror work when I began writing this book and then it fell away until I got to this chapter. So, I started it again.

Embrace Your Awesomeness

Get up tomorrow, look in the mirror and tell yourself you love the person looking back.

Now you have embarked on bringing back the love, see how you can allow certainty into your life—the right way.

CHALLENGES

Try these challenges for the next 30 days and then decide which ones you want to continue with for the long term.

Challenge 1 – Awesomeness pep talk: read the awesomeness pep talk to yourself once per day.

Challenge 2 – Self-love affirmations: say self-love affirmations to yourself in the mirror for one minute per day.

Challenge 3 – Practice self-care: make a list of your favorite self-care activities and commit to doing at least one per day.

Bonus 'Anytime' Challenge – Decide on your go-to extravagant compliment. Write it down and say it out loud three times whenever you are being critical of yourself.

8

SECURITY AND CONTROL

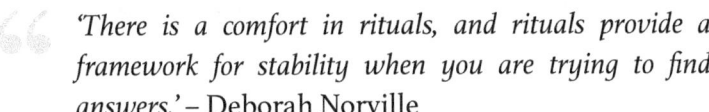

'There is a comfort in rituals, and rituals provide a framework for stability when you are trying to find answers.' – Deborah Norville

THE CASE OF THE MISSING KINDERGARTEN FAREWELL

When the pandemic lockdown came in March 2020, it was swift and stringent. Kids were sent to school on a Monday like normal and by the end of the day they were told to go home and not come back for at least a month.

Unfortunately for my daughter, Eloise, the lockdown put her in a predicament, a no-mans-land between kindergarten and school. She was turning five in a few weeks which means, here in New Zealand, that she was due to finish up at kindy and go to school. In the end, she started school two weeks later than planned, not a big deal in the scheme of things. What was extremely upsetting for me (thankfully not so much for my daughter), was that Eloise didn't get to have her kindergarten farewell celebration.

I know this doesn't seem like a major concern, what with a deadly global pandemic to worry about. But of all the things that the strict quarantine caused, my daughter not being able to say goodbye properly to her kindergarten family is what kept me awake at night. A few years back, my son, Dylan, was able to make his crown, blow out the candles on his mini-birthday cake and get the 'happy birthday' and 'happy school days' songs sung at his farewell. I even have faded photos of my own kindergarten goodbye.

Luckily, after Eloise started school, we arranged for her to skip out early one Friday and go back to kindergarten to say goodbye properly. It was a wonderful celebration, complete with crown, cake and songs. To be honest, Eloise was impartial about it, fully engaged in school already, but I absolutely needed it, for the sake of a good night's sleep, if nothing else.

Finding Positive Ways to Be in Control

Finding ways to feel in control of your life is vitally important. As we have seen, striving for too much certainty has its downsides, but taking the reins helps you feel safe. In fact, feeling in control of your life is proven to be linked with more success, health and happiness. We just need to figure out how to do it the right way.

The first thing that helps is understanding that there are tons of things that we have complete control over.

Here is a small selection:

- Mindset – your thoughts, beliefs, emotions, attitude, opinions, perspective
- Values – how honest you are, how much gratitude you express

- Activities – the books you read, sports you play, hobbies you take up
- Social – choice of friends, asking for help, how kind you want to be
- Food – what food you put in your mouth, how often and when you eat
- Decisions – level of risk you take on, whether to try something new or retry
- Language – what you say, how you say it, when to just shut up and listen
- Body – how often you smile, move, stretch, dance or sing
- Money – how much you earn, spend and save
- Work – what work you do, how much effort you put in
- Sleep – the time you go to bed, when you turn out the lights

I get it. Some of these things may sound confronting and not at all in your control. Maybe you don't feel like you can change jobs, save the money you want or have time for exercise or sleep. Just because right now these may seem impossible doesn't mean you don't have control over them. Life is full of stages with varying degrees of control in different areas. Parents of a newborn may not be able to choose when they sleep—believe me, I know! But one day your child will sleep through the night—hallelujah—and you will too again.

Please just start to entertain the notion that you have much more influence and power over your life than the constant barrage of news, social media and others' opinions will have you believe. If author and holocaust survivor Victor Frankl believes it, you can too. His most enduring insight is that forces beyond your control can take away everything except for your freedom to choose how you will respond to a situation.

> You can control what you think, feel and do about what happens to you.

Empowerment occurs with choice. You will always have problems, so aim for better problems! You can choose to believe something and also change your mind. When something happens, knowing you have control over whether to accept it, leave it or change it helps a lot. Remember, it doesn't matter if it is 'true', only that it is helpful.

What kept me from having a peaceful slumber when we were unsure if the kindergarten farewell event would happen was that the lockdown left an 'open loop'. Open loops occur mundanely on a daily basis and are such a seamless part of the fabric of life you barely notice them. You text someone, you put on a load of washing, you wait for the train. But if the loops aren't closed, anxiety creeps in. He never texts back, the washing machine breaks down, the train is late. One constructive way to feel in control, and reduce stress, is to close as many open loops as you can.

Here are three other, positive ways to create security and control:

- Rituals and Habits
- Empowering Language
- Tap into Your Intuition

RITUALS AND HABITS

Habits, systems, routines, traditions, customs or rituals create certainty in both positive and negative ways. You can take up smoking or take up running and you can be certain of one thing —each will have a different outcome. I prefer the term 'ritual' as it has an enlightened ring to it, but the words will be used interchangeably in this section.

Last night, five-year-old Eloise started crying and pointing at the piece of broccoli on her dinner plate. While wiping away tears, we ascertained that she was annoyed that everyone at the table got MORE broccoli than her. She wanted her fair share. Yes, she wanted extra broccoli! When I wrote about making eating vegetables a habit in *Easy Peasy Healthy Eating*, I installed it as a fixture in my own home. Every night just before dinner the kids are offered a bowl of raw vegetables. On their actual dinner plates, they often have some salad or cooked greens. Sometimes they eat them all up and ask for more. Other evenings I am told emphatically that they no longer eat carrots. In the long run, they eat a lot more vegetables, and enjoy them too, than if I hadn't started this practice.

Habits have so many benefits in addition to giving us a sense of control and predictability. People erroneously think habits deny freedom but they actually provide more freedom as they give us space to make other decisions and think creatively. They also convey a sense of mastery as doing a habit over time will improve how well you perform. If you install the routine in your life, if it is something you just do, the ingrained habit minimizes perfectionism and procrastination. Last, habits eliminate the need for willpower and discipline. If it is part of your lifestyle, then you don't need to push yourself to do it. It just happens.

Selecting and increasing the number of positive habits not only helps you feel in control but changes your life for the better. Identifying and reducing bad habits is equally important. How do you go about this? You build a habit in four steps: a cue to notice and initiate behavior, a craving to change your state and get what you want, your response which is the habit you perform, and the reward or the goal that satisfies your craving. If you want to floss every night, for example, the cue is brushing your teeth, the craving is a clean mouth feel, the response is the actual flossing and the reward is a gold star from your dentist. You are more likely to do this if the floss is next to the toothpaste and you have built it into your nightly routine. I urge you to read James Clear's wonderful book, *Atomic Habits* for a full breakdown and many examples. Don't have time for reading? Make it a habit, say 15 minutes before lights out each night.

What you want to do is identify habits that provide more certainty, that give you a feeling you are in control of your life and then make them as simple as possible. As James Clear states, "redesign your life so the actions that matter most are also the actions that are easiest to do." The self-love affirmation and self-care practices introduced in the last chapter are exactly the kind of rituals you want to make easy.

Here are two more examples:

Rituals and Traditions: Rituals and traditions feel both personal and profound. We try to eat dinner as a family most nights and when we do, we pause for a few seconds to say thank you. This is a general thank you to the food producers, the stores, whoever cooked that night and the fact we get to sit at the dinner table and have a meal together. Work out some rituals and traditions that are meaningful and install them into your life. When the world is banana-pants crazy, rituals and traditions help you feel settled.

Practical Systems: Although not so magical, dealing with practical areas of your life makes everything easier. Practices can be yearly, monthly, weekly, daily or more often. Schedule in the calendar once per year to review your life paperwork—your will, insurances and family budget. Decide on weekly meal plans. Block out a daily movement time. Make your bed each morning. Look at your own life and see where you can automate decisions and reduce friction so life doesn't feel so out of control. None of

Embrace Your Awesomeness

this has to be hard. Do you know how I make sure I don't lose this manuscript draft? No back up, no app, no cloud. I press save, close the document and send it to myself in an email.

Empowering Language

You are in control of whether you speak at all plus every single word that comes out of your mouth. You wanted control. Isn't it amazing how much certainty we can gain in the area of language?

Unfortunately, many of us have habitually ingrained a number of disempowering words and phrases. We use a lot of negative sounding words: 'must', 'have to', 'need to' and that perennial favorite 'should' that imply that we don't have options in our lives. This is a language of disempowerment, of busy, stressed, exhausted people who have forgotten that they have choices. We need to first be aware of this and then stop it. These are just stories we tell ourselves; they are not necessarily true and they are definitely not helpful.

Consciously reworking what you say into empowering language increases how much you feel in control of your life. Find replacement words and say them instead.

Here are some positive switches to start you off:

- I have to -> I get to
- I must -> I prefer to
- I need to -> I choose to
- Can't -> Won't
- Hope -> Know
- Never -> Lately
- Should -> Could
- Always -> Sometimes
- Problem -> Opportunity

- Just, actually, kind of -> I would like

Yes, it seems like you must take the kids to school, have to make their lunches and should get to school on time, but just play with it a bit. Try on the empowering language, say it out loud, see how it feels. You prefer to take the kids to school, get to make their lunches and could get to school on time. It may feel a bit strange but is it any less true?

How to start? Building on the habits section above, make it easy by changing one phrase at a time, perhaps the worst one in your vocabulary. Maybe 'should' and its implication that you are wrong is the one that needs to go. Also, associate positive feelings with using this new form of language. You don't have to sound stern or like a robot. Use these new empowering phrases with all the warmth and good humor you can muster.

Tap into Your Intuition

I had some books to return so I hopped in the car to make a quick trip to the local library. Just before I backed out of the garage, without any conscious thought, I got out of the car and walked around to the rear of it. Eloise, who was about two at the time, and a few seconds before had been playing out in the backyard, was standing directly behind the car. I simply wouldn't have seen her if I had backed out as I usually did. What could have happened is too horrific for me to contemplate. Sure, maybe I saw her walk by out of the corner of my eye, or perhaps heard a noise I didn't entirely register. But I would like to believe that it was my intuition that directed me to check behind my car that day.

Intuition may seem like an odd choice to help you feel more in control, but please hear me out. First, before I explain why tapping into your intuition helps increase certainty, I want to say that it is only one tool in the toolbox. Use it in addition to other tools such as practical actions and routines. After the car incident, we put a double lock on the internal garage door and made sure we shut it every time we went out.

Intuition is poorly understood and surrounded by myths and half-truths. It's simply a knowing beyond words—the ability to understand something without conscious reasoning. Whether you believe it or not, everyone has an intuitive side. Some are more in touch with it than others. Yours is in there somewhere! It can be difficult to decipher lizard brain chatter from intuition so know that your gut won't speak to you in actual words. Instead it calmly whispers to you via your physical sensations, in dreams, having unexpected energy or pain or in strange synchronicities. It moves you in the right direction but doesn't tell you your destination, which is why it doesn't link up with that 'closed loop' feeling that you traditionally need to feel secure. When I got out of my car, I was compelled to walk behind it, even though I didn't know why. I didn't feel anxious. It was actually one of the calmest feelings I ever had until I saw Eloise standing there.

Getting back to listening to your intuition is not something to learn, but to unlearn—you must make space for it. First, practice leaning away from the need to logically make decisions and rationalize. Allow the possibility that your intuition is as good as, if not better than your frontal lobe. Second, get back in touch with your body. It's called a 'gut reaction' for a reason. Anything that strengthens the core helps with your intuition. Straighten up your posture and take some deep belly breaths throughout the day. Do this now—sit or stand up straight and take four deep breaths, expanding your stomach on the inhale and blowing out on the exhale. Last, add in a daily stillness habit: pause to breathe deeply, walk in nature, meditate or simply sit in silence and notice your five physical senses. These all help to give your lizard brain a rest and let your intuition speak.

Along with more control, a willingness to trust your intuition is associated with overcoming self-doubt, greater ease and flow and more happiness and success. There is so much more that could be said on intuition, its benefits and how to tap into it, but this section is a taster to help you pivot your understanding and to allow it some room in your busy life.

Your intuition is always, always, always, working for you.

You want certainty and it is inside of you, at the core of you, at all times. What could make you feel more secure than that?

The next chapter helps enhance the only area of your life proven to be directly linked to your happiness—your relationships.

CHALLENGES

Try these challenges for the next 30 days and then decide which ones you want to continue with for the long term.

Challenge 1 – Rituals and habits: decide to do one positive habit every day for the next month, e.g.: go for a 20-minute walk, have a bowl of raw vegetables before dinner, say thanks at every mealtime, make your bed or spend some time reading.

Challenge 2 – Empowering language: change at least one disempowering word or phrase to an empowering one, e.g.: remove 'should' from your vocabulary. Simply don't say those negative words. The Lizard might still think them, but don't say them out loud. I doubt anyone will notice as they are too busy rushing around being stressed. But you will feel a difference.

Challenge 3 – Tap into your intuition: add in a daily stillness habit: pause, breathe deeply, walk in nature, meditate or sit in silence and notice your five physical senses in order to make space for you to tap into your intuition.

Bonus 'Anytime' Challenge – Adopt some practical habits you want to set up and continue with on, say, a monthly basis, e.g.: reviewing your expenses, installing a regular date night or volunteering.

9

SOCIAL AWESOMENESS

 'There is only one way to avoid criticism: do nothing, say nothing, and be nothing.' – Aristotle

OPRAH SAYS NO

I attended a live show with Oprah Winfrey a few years ago. She talked for almost three hours, imparting many life lessons and vibrant wisdom. One time, Stevie Wonder asked her to help out on a project he was coordinating. She was very busy with other priorities but didn't want to let her friend down or be thought of as a bad person (who identifies with this?). After days of hand-wringing, she called Stevie Wonder back and said that she couldn't assist him at this time. She expected the worst. What was the response? A simple 'no problem' from the singer. Oprah explained to the 10,000-strong audience that that was the day she learned that 'no' is a complete sentence.

. . .

Boundaries

No one has yet proven that money, career choice or—unbelievably—even health, have much of an effect on how happy you are. But consistently, across many different studies, personal connections and strong social bonds have been shown to make a meaningful contribution to happiness.

Why then do our primary relationships often steer us to anger, sadness, stress and chaos? Our lizard brains, the fear that we are not enough and an excruciating need to feel loved at any cost lead to behaviors that drive away real connection. Without true bonds, our relationships function on a surface level, but the joy we seek is smothered by our poor attempts to feel safe and secure.

Paradoxically, the way to allow ourselves to be more empathetic and vulnerable in our relationships is to install strong boundaries. Brené Brown says, "Compassionate people ask for what they need. They say no when they need to, and when they say 'yes', they mean it. They're compassionate because their boundaries keep them out of resentment."

Boundaries don't constrain us, they free us.

Boundaries are simply the line where we separate ourselves from others. You can install new boundaries, uphold existing ones and move them when they no longer suit you. They can arise in many different areas including around time, money, work, thoughts, emotions and physical space. For instance, if you allow people to directly influence your feelings or you take action that prevents others from being in touch with emotions, your boundaries need to be reviewed. You are not responsible for anyone else's happiness, sadness or any other feeling. This is such a simple concept to understand but so hard to put into practice. Especially as a mama, I want my kids to feel content. However, if we take this to its logical conclusion, my eight-year-old, Dylan, would feel most happy eating ice cream and playing Minecraft all day long.

> **Boundaries done right allow people to grow into their best selves.**

If they are so important, why don't we uphold them? Like Oprah experienced, we are worried about what the other person will think, want to avoid potential conflict and want to be thought of as a nice person. These are fears directed by our lizard brains and are perfectly normal, but they can be overcome. It's your choice: discomfort or resentment?

This chapter provides three boundary-related tools to increase connection. Done correctly, boundaries make you feel safe and in control of your life. They are another form of self-care in action. In addition, these tools help you to maintain great social interactions that keep your budding self-love, self-respect and self-worth intact.

Here are three boundary tools:

- Say 'No'
- Detach from Approval and Criticism
- Better Communication

Say 'No'

Building and upholding boundaries is such a large topic that it is easy to feel overwhelmed. Where do you start? You start by saying 'no'.

Saying 'no' after a lifetime of 'yes' will be difficult, at least at first. It takes practice and commitment. But if you do not learn to say 'no', then you are saying 'yes' to someone else's agenda and 'no' to yourself.

If you are unsure whether to say 'no' to a future commitment, ask yourself if you would do that very thing tomorrow. Tomorrow is probably already booked up solid, so if you still want to do that thing, then say 'yes', otherwise say 'no'. Remember that you never, ever want to offer a begrudging 'yes' when your gut is saying 'no'. Author and entrepreneur, Derek Sivers, says, "If you're not saying HELL YEAH! about something, say NO."

Even in the nicest way possible, saying 'no' is uncomfortable, so practice on small things and build up. Here are a few ways to say 'no' politely:

- "I apologize but that doesn't work for me."
- "Sorry but my current commitments mean I cannot take that on."
- "I can't help you at the moment but I can schedule it after X date."
- "Sounds wonderful, but that is not part of my work focus right now."
- "It sounds amazing but I wouldn't be able to give that the attention it deserves."
- "Sorry it is not my policy to do X." (People respect policies, even ones you have made up yourself!)

Another tip is to say, "Let me check my diary and I will come back to you." This gives you a buffer, a soft no. Make sure you do respond promptly, whether in the affirmative or negative. Suggesting someone else to assist also helps soften the no blow: "Connor in accounts would be the best help for that."

Occasionally, offering your no with humor works. When my children ask me something ridiculous like if they can drive the car, a simple "Nope!" is sufficient.

If a no is done well, people should be happy with how clear and committed you are to what is important to you. And if they are not happy? Well, their response is their problem. Unfortunately, unlike with Oprah, sometimes the other party will respond in an attacking or negative way to your no. This doesn't happen as much as you think it might, but the possibility is there. Hold your ground! What you are doing is moving a boundary line and it is normal for the other person to not like this. After all, things then seem out of their control. But if it is important to you, gently but firmly reiterate your no response. Brené Brown says that she has not regretted increasing boundaries or a single no. The other party will soon accept the new normal or move on to someone more amenable. More on assertive communication and uncoupling from what others think in the next sections.

DETACH FROM APPROVAL AND CRITICISM

Wanting approval, appreciation, recognition, praise and compliments and avoiding criticism, rejection and conflict are deeply ingrained needs. Dale Carnegie summed it up best in the self-help classic, *How to Win Friends and Influence People*: "As much as we thirst for approval, we dread condemnation." We think we are not enough so look externally for validation. We may be met with brickbats or bouquets, but in either case we are giving away our power and control to something outside of ourselves.

I really dislike the advice to grow a thicker skin. The whole visual of a crusty casing, a hard-shell outer layer is kind of repulsive to me. How do we navigate social relationships that have the potential to wound without growing an exoskeleton?

First, we cultivate self-love using all the tools described above. We practice loving affirmations. We value being authentic. We take up self-care in all its forms. Next, we develop habits and other positive ways to feel in control. We initiate and hold boundaries. And then we can choose to take a step out of our comfort zones and let approval go in favor of being real.

Next time you want approval or are trying to avoid criticism, use these reminders to quickly get out of your own way:

- Focus on results, not approval
- Say a simple 'thanks' whatever the opinion
- Know that somebody out there needs your message or your gifts
- Don't judge or limit yourself when you don't know what others are thinking
- Consider that no one recalls what was said yesterday, chiefly on the socials
- Understand that what others think of you has nothing to do with you and everything to do with them

Building on boundaries, the most effective way to detach from others' opinions is to decide on exactly what topics, situations and people you care about. Straight away, this eliminates all strangers on and offline, especially anonymous commenters on the socials. It also omits any topic you don't care about. If like me, you are not interested in college sports or fixing up old motorbikes, simply don't engage. Any situation in which the person with the opinion has little to no knowledge on a topic can be disregarded. I don't need a friend in financial trouble giving me stock trading tips. This may not help with specific approval and rejection per se, but it does start to build up your boundaries around who you let into your inner sanctum.

This does leave you open to the opinion of someone who you respect or who is very close to you. In the past, I was stung so hard by rejection, I didn't know which way was up. It is especially hard to take criticism if it matches some negative belief about yourself—you are not thin / smart / rich enough, that kind of thing. Strengthening your self-love muscle is always a first step.

A profound way to manage in these situations is to pivot—make it very easy to feel approval and extremely hard to feel criticism. Approval occurs almost 24/7 in my life. Whenever I express gratitude, smile or take a deep breath I feel approval. I am in charge of my own appreciation because, well, I love me and I'm awesome. I like praise and recognition from others but as the cherry on top of my ice-cream sundae. As I said earlier, I absolutely adore every five-star book review, but I would still write these books regardless.

Now, rejection happens ONLY if I were to consistently believe the false illusion that the world is mean, that everything has to be in order and that others have the power to reject me instead of knowing deep in my soul that the world has an endless abundance of love, energy and joy, that the only thing I have to do is breathe and I am the only one who determines how I feel in any moment.

I take on personal, specific, well-thought-out feedback and discard the rest. Why would I waste my precious time otherwise?

A meaningful way to drop the need for others to think well of you is to commit to a cause or venture that is much bigger than yourself. When Dylan started at a daycare close to my workplace in the city, I noticed that there was a walkway immediately adjacent to the outside play space that workers from nearby offices used as a smoking area during their breaks. Not wanting my beautiful baby boy (and all the other kids) to play in second-hand smoke, I immediately called the daycare supervisor, the building manager and the local council to see what could be done to erect 'No Smoking' signs in the walkway as soon as possible. I am sure a number of people I interacted with thought I was being dramatic / bossy / an overprotective mama, but all that mattered to me was that the cigarette smoking directly outside the daycare stopped immediately. Within a week, 'No Smoking' signs were up and my baby was playing in clean(er) air. You get to decide if being creative, inspiring, completing a challenge or contributing on a greater scale is more important than being liked.

You have installed some much-needed boundaries via the practice of saying 'no' and restricting the situations where approval or criticism can bite you. No focus on social relationships would be complete without a look at communication.

Better Communication

Communication is a gateway to building connections, developing deeper relationships and feeling secure in them... if you get it right.

Did those suggestions of how to say 'no' politely give you a slightly sick feeling? Reread them again. Practice saying them out loud. Despite what you are led to believe, the statements are not aggressive, bossy or rude. Assuming your tone and volume is reasonable, they can only be described as warm, direct and assertive. Your objective is to up your level of warm, direct and assertive communication and reduce other forms. This is a win-win as it suggests care for both parties: me AND you. This helps you feel in control and presents your most compassionate self to the world.

There are four main types of spoken communication, best explained using examples. What is the response when a colleague asks you for your assistance on his task when you have a full load to finish today and would like to leave work on time?

- Passive: "Ok, no problem." (While seething inside).
- Passive-Aggressive: "Ok, no problem. I'll just stay late as usual."
- Aggressive: "What? No way. And don't ask me again."
- Assertive 1: "No." (It really is a complete sentence!)
- Assertive 2: "Sorry, no. I am leaving on time today. I may have a spare half-hour to help you tomorrow after lunch."

Hopefully it is obvious that assertive communication is the goal. Here are some other examples of warm, direct, assertive communication in close relationships:

- I statements: "I feel like..." rather than "You made me feel..."
- Consequences: "Please make your bed or you are not playing Minecraft"
- Ask for what you want: "Please buy milk on the way home..." rather than "We are out of milk again, why do I have to sort this out every time?"

Keeping warm, direct and assertive in your mind bodes well in all communication but especially when you have to have a tough conversation. Embracing your awesomeness means standing your ground while being as empathetic as you can. Even if resentment or frustration may seem easier, tough conversations can no longer be avoided. They are likely to be painful. But the alternative is numbing, evading and not living life to the fullest, and I, for one, am not prepared to continue along that path any longer.

It is worth noting that one of the top five regrets of the dying was 'I wish I'd had the courage to express my feelings.' Assertive communication is a great way to do this. Harriet Lerner writes in *The Dance of Anger*, using the phrase, "I am not criticizing you, just telling you how I feel and what I want" is not easy to say but a very good place to start. This may make the other person feel more out of control and emotional. Let them feel their feelings. Don't deny them the experience of moving through their own pain. Yes, tough stuff, but growth is always better than stagnation.

Becoming more assertive does not mean becoming more argumentative. Upholding or moving boundaries often leads to what is termed 'change-back attacks'. Arguments for the most part end up with both sides being more certain of their own points of view. Essentially, our need for certainty trumps our need for love. If you strive to convince the other that they are wrong how does that help build a better relationship?

Why choose to be right instead of happy when there is no way to be right?

Instead, thank the person for bringing the point to your attention, muster all the calmness you can, listen to them fully and try not to jump in to defend yourself. Tell the other party that you want to think over their point and if you can, show them some appreciation for having a strong interest. You may not feel like doing this, but if the relationship is important to you, then it is the more loving thing to do. As Dale Carnegie says, most people want sympathy so challenge yourself to offer friendliness irrespective of what is said. Using the phrase "tell me more" when it is the very last thing you want to hear is a courageous act.

Win-Win

Better communication means warmly, directly and assertively speaking up for what you want and what is important to you. It is self-love in action. And it means avoiding unimportant arguments, being friendly and saying less for the sake of your relationships—love for others in the real world. Navigating these life paradoxes is not easy but there is no other way to play a win-win game in the social arena.

Empathy and compassion require you to understand and agree with other's pain. They do not require you to take it on, to load yourself up with it, to wear it as a t-shirt. The only way you can increase your understanding, empathy and compassion, which is what this banana-pants crazy world needs desperately, is to combine self-love and acceptance with strong boundaries.

Understand or try to comprehend what they are feeling but don't feel it for them. You have the right to everything you think and feel AND so does everyone else. I am the first to admit that it can be easier to sit in resentment and judgement but it is far more fulfilling to try and believe that everyone is doing the best they can with what they have and love them no matter what. At the end of the day it's all love.

Love is ALWAYS the answer even when we don't want it to be.

Throughout this book, I have mentioned the top five regrets of the dying from book of the same name. They reflect what happens at the end of our lives when we let our lizard brain fear and need for certainty take over. So far, we have:

- I wish I hadn't worked so hard
- I wish I had let myself be happier
- I wish I'd had the courage to express my feelings
- I wish I had had the courage to live a life true to myself, not the life others expected of me

The final one is 'I wish I had stayed in touch with my friends'.

What could possibly be more important than nurturing relationships in the most win-win way possible?

Let's move onto the fourth and last solution. It is the final one for a reason as it asks you to face uncertainty head on.

CHALLENGES

Try these challenges for the next 30 days and then decide which ones you want to continue with for the long term.

Challenge 1 – Say 'no': say a polite 'no' every day—to your partner, kids, friends, work colleagues, charities, committees, sales people and anyone else who comes along. Remember 'no' is a complete sentence.

Challenge 2 – Detach from approval and criticism: practice ignoring opinions of those who do not matter (95% of the world) and saying a simple 'thanks' to any other feedback you receive in the next month.

Challenge 3 – Better communication: be vigilant at reworking as much of your communication as possible into warm, direct and assertive sentences, using I statements, consequences and asking for exactly what you want.

Bonus 'Anytime' Challenge – Use the phrase 'tell me more' when it is the very last thing you want to do during a tough conversation or argument.

10

STEP OUT OF YOUR COMFORT ZONE

> *"And you ask 'What if I fall?'*
>
> *Oh but my darling,*
>
> *what if you fly?"* – Erin Hanson

BOATY MCBOATFACE

In 2016, a British government agency asked the public to suggest a name for a new polar research ship. Appropriate names such as Endeavor and Falcon for the grand and expensive vessel were put aside when an out-of-the-box proposition became the clear front-runner. All the good people of the Internet wanted the ship, which was commissioned to carry out serious scientific exploration, to be called Boaty McBoatface.

In the end, the ship was named the R.S.S Sir David Attenborough after the natural historian. The powers-that-be did concede to the general public's whim and gave the name Boaty McBoatface to a small autonomous submarine in their fleet.

You may think this story is a red, flashing, neon warning sign against letting chaos rein. But it is the complete opposite. It illustrates just how creative, light-hearted and community-spirited humans can be when they are invited to imagine, dream and step out of their comfort zones. Isn't that what we want more of in the world?

Forecast: Uncertainty

The last few chapters have demonstrated that there is a great deal that you are in control of and that you can establish practices and habits to increase certainty over your life even further. Ultimately, though, there is and always will be an awful lot that is never going to be within your control. As the Serenity Prayer so eloquently puts it: 'Grant me the serenity to accept the things I cannot change, the courage to change the things I can, and the wisdom to know the difference.' You can check the weather forecast and take an umbrella with you but you can't stop the rain.

People don't want to leave their comfort zone as it feels pleasant and familiar, and they feel safe and in control of their environments. Going to work, coming home, watching TV, these are all nice at times. Being in your comfort zone is comfortable, but after a while it starts to hurt you. You start to feel unenthused and jaded with your routine existence.

Right now, with the pandemic going on, you may really feel like your comfort zone is the one thing you can hold onto, that you need it to survive, to just get through each day. I get it. Please don't embark on the solutions and tools in this chapter if you are barely holding your head above the water. Keep going with the self-love practices, establishing habits that make you feel more in control and deepen relationships with those close to you. When you are ready, come back here.

However, in order to live with insecurity without hiding away under a rock, you need to find ways to feel okay even when you are not in control. You need to step out of your comfort zone. This takes courage and you can't have courage and comfort at the same time. Trying new things leads to growth, and growth is necessary for a fulfilling life. Studies have shown over and over again that successful people make a habit of being uncomfortable.

You have already started to do this by attempting challenges such as self-love affirmations, tapping into your intuition and practicing saying 'no'. You have started to embrace the notion that determining if something is helpful is better than fighting for the 'truth'. You really do have agency over your decisions and can change things.

Just outside of your comfort zone is where the magic is.

Susan Jeffers sums this up elegantly in *Embracing Uncertainty*: "I relax my consciousness. I un-set my heart. I wear the world as a loose garment. I learn to dance with grace on the constantly shifting carpet."

Here are three tools to step out of—and ultimately expand—your comfort zone:

- Fail
- Create
- Dream Big

Fail

In *Super Sexy Goal Setting*, I stated my goals for the year in a book I wrote about how to write and achieve your goals, and I didn't accomplish them. I didn't just fail, but failed publicly! This is the most mortifying kind of failure.

In an attempt to recover from my failure-induced despondency I did a little digging. My research found me in good company. Many successful people have encountered failure. I can now see failure can be a rich, meaningful and, dare I say, agreeable, experience. I encourage you to fail for three reasons:

1. Failure Is a Chance to Learn What Doesn't Work

When billionaire business owner, Sara Blakely, was a child, her father would ask her over dinner what she had failed at that week. If she didn't have something to report, he was disappointed. To him, if his children weren't failing, they weren't trying.

Perhaps only half a book is written by the deadline, or the side business only makes a few dollars or the finish line is crossed well after everyone else has gone home. So what? It still means that you did better than everyone who never tried. You can do it again and do it better. You learned a lot, gained skills, and now you know what to focus on to improve next time. If you shoot for the stars and only land on the moon, you can still be proud of what you achieved.

2. Failing Is The Only Way to Get Over the Fear

Understandably, stepping out of your comfort zone is associated with a fear of failure. One way to get over that is to expect it. You will fail. Sometimes you will fall down so spectacularly hard that you are not sure if your tailbone will ever feel right again. But you will also learn to get back up, dust yourself off and keep going.

Once you fail and survive, the fear loses its grip a bit. You learn, as Sara Blakely says, "failure is not the outcome". The fear will make you think that failure means the end but it is only the beginning. Maybe next time you will fail better.

3. THE MOST SUCCESSFUL PEOPLE HAVE FAILED

All the most successful people have failed. Failed big time. This list may help you feel better about your failures:

- Oprah Winfrey was fired from her first TV job at a local news station as she was 'unfit for television'.
- J.K. Rowling's *Harry Potter* manuscript was rejected by all 12 major publishers.
- Elvis Presley failed an audition to become part of a vocalist quartet as he was told he 'couldn't sing'.
- Walt Disney was fired from his newspaper job because he 'lacked imagination and had no good ideas'.
- Michael Jordan, at 15, was passed up for his high school basketball team.

Your true character is built not on whether you failed but on how and when you pick yourself back up again. Embracing failure is the antidote for perfectionism, procrastination and playing small. You can't be perfect if you fail. Why chronically procrastinate when trying and possibly failing are something to look forward to? Giving it a go is great for building confidence and strengthening your self-esteem and thus playing a bigger game.

. . .

Creativity

Best-selling author, Elizabeth Gilbert said in her *Magic Lessons* podcast that creativity is an irrational act. Essentially you are saying that you are going to take the single most valuable commodity you have—the irreplaceable currency of time—and devote it to making something that nobody wants, that nobody asked you to do, that nobody is waiting for, that might not work, and that you might not even like. Why in the world would you do that?

I have some answers to that deep question and they revolve around writing a novel in a month. In November 2016, I wrote my very first novel during National Novel Writing Month. This is a mouthful so it gets abbreviated to NaNoWriMo, which really is only slightly less of a mouthful. Each year, in November, thousands of writers around the world take up the challenge to write a 50,000-word (approximately 180 page) novel for NaNoWriMo. I can now count myself as a NaNoWriMo 'winner'. Winners succeed in getting 50,000 words written before the end of the month. Other participants have varying levels of success up to that lofty number. The point is to ignore your inner editor and plough on. Just get those words down. My silly little romance may never be seen by anyone else but it more or less contained elements that make it a complete—albeit draft—work of fiction.

So why create? Here are three reasons:

1. To try something that seems far too ambitious, ridiculous or pointless. Deciding to embark on a hard, challenging or passion-fueled task is often surprisingly fulfilling. It taps into that inner child in all of us.

2. To get into the 'flow state'. This is what humans want and need more of, and it is becoming increasingly rare these days with constant distractions only a tap of the finger away. In the throes of

creativity, you can't help but be in flow, be really present. And it feels amazing.

3. To start something. It is perfectly okay to start something with absolutely no idea of how the process will go, how it should look or how on earth you are going to finish it. Trusting the creative process means letting yourself be pleasantly surprised by where the project takes you. I am a very organized person and thought I would have a perfect outline and screeds of character notes before I started NaNoWriMo. In fact, all I did was draw a giant mind map which I then proceeded to ignore and allowed my characters to take on a life of their own.

Like intuition, everyone is creative, but some people have lost their sense of it. You can relearn to be creative. Historical data shows that people are less depressed and have higher confidence the more they use their hands.

Try any or all of the following to strengthen your creativity muscle: cook, draw, paint, knit, sew, build, write songs, dance, decorate, make videos, brew beer, make soap, take up photography or of course, write a novel. Creativity is only limited by your imagination.

Creativity is not self-indulgent or trivial. It is one of the most important things we can do for ourselves and the planet. It reflects our awesomeness as creating stems from our uniqueness. Charles Pépin write in *Self-Confidence: A Philosophy* that "our thumbs glide over the surface of smart phones and we glide over the surface of things." We are not present in our bodies, not in touch with our senses anymore. If going within is too woo-woo for you, then here is your answer: create something tangible. It is reassuring to make, master or finish something. The sourdough and banana bread baking trends during quarantine make complete sense.

Creativity allows us to meet ourselves once again.

And if those reasons above don't encourage you to create, then don't do it for yourself. Do it for others. You never know who your project will touch so don't give up on it. Just do it. Because I embraced my creativity and wrote a book, I was invited onto a virtual summit with a number of other women from different fields. A friend of mine, Georgie, inspired as a result of watching another interview, decided to start her own creative venture. As a thank you, she gave me a gorgeous crystal bracelet that she now makes as part of her business, Elegant Empowerment. Think about this for a second. I wrote a book and somewhere along the way, this helped someone to start a business. Please don't deny your creativity for another second.

DREAM BIG

To dream big is to make every piece of your life the masterpiece it is meant to be because it doesn't matter how great your life is, there is another level—one of passion, gratitude, connection, joy and success.

Dreaming big is the very last awesomeness tool. It has purposely been left until last because you need to get a handle on the other tools before you truly adopt this one. Everything learned to date assists with dreaming big. You can't dream big if you are stuck in your immediate pleasure-seeking response and have no boundaries. Dreaming big means saying 'no' to something good now for the bigger prize later. And it won't happen unless you adore yourself and know you deserve a huge life simply because you are alive. Dreams will remain dreams unless you choose courage over comfort.

Desire has some funny connotations and seems controversial, but we all have desires and it is imperative we work out exactly what we want and go for it. Our need for certainty drops with every step out of our comfort zone and the world is richer as a result of our boldness.

Don't settle for mediocrity because you believe anything else is unavailable or inappropriate. Be rebellious. See what you can get away with. Not many people's opinions matter. So why not? When you go beyond expectations and what you think you are capable of, the world will open up. You will discover there is so much more you can do with your mind, body, skills and talents. You may even compel others to dream big too.

The best way to initiate dreaming big is to set yourself an audacious challenge. This appeals to an innate desire to excel, helps get you unstuck and taps into your best self. One morning, not long after I turned 39, I woke and up with a ridiculous idea: I could attempt to check off 40 bucket list items in the following year to mark my 40th birthday milestone.

My 'Top40 Bucket List' was born. Some items were cheap, local, and even dull. 'Grow sunflowers' was one item that would seem modest to others. Some I had to plan and budget for—traveling to another city to see 'The World of Wearable Arts' was one of the more expensive and time-consuming items. I definitely had to consider finances, family commitments and other constraints, but I had a list of 40 bucket list items I was intent on checking off. What a way to commemorate turning 40!

And as I write in *Bucket List Blueprint*, I did succeed in checking off every single one of the 40 bucket list items during that year. I ended on a literal high note when on the 30th of December, I jumped out of a plane in a tandem skydive. Doing my Top40 Bucket List was a mighty challenge, stressful and hard work at times, but I still feel extremely proud and satisfied that I crossed it all off.

Right now, with travel restrictions in place, this may seem like an impossible challenge. However, you can do a whole lot of stuff at home or in your local area. And nothing is stopping you from writing a bucket list for later. It doesn't even have to be a list. Name one challenge you would like to try before you 'kick the bucket' and start planning to make it happen.

Celebration

You have dreamed big, been creative, and, er, failed—now go and celebrate! Celebrating is another way of stepping out of your comfort zone. It can be tremendously fun as long as you don't allow your fear of what others may think of your 'bragging' to get in the way. It is also a way to pause and reflect and we all need a breather now and then. You need to celebrate YOU. If you don't, who else will? Repeat after me: "No one is going to give you a medal." Feel free to insert an expletive word before medal if you like. Remember, you are awesome! At the very least, celebrate your birthday.

A really fun way to celebrate is to spend a few minutes listing your accomplishments, challenges you have faced and your acts of kindness. All of them. Big and small. Over your whole life. That third place in long jump in the fifth grade. Managing to play that tricky piano solo in front of your grandmother. That first pay check. The university degree. Having a baby. Downsizing and traveling the world. Standing up for something you believe in. Telling someone you love them. Writing a note of thanks about your favorite waiter. Large successes such as climbing a mountain, writing a book or designing your dream home. Smaller, yet no less significant accomplishments such as getting out of bed and taking a shower when you were in the midst of a dark time. Write them all down. It will be a long list. Refer back to it often and give yourself a pat on the back or perform a little dance of joy every time you read it.

One thing you can celebrate is almost getting to the end of this book—only two short chapters to go.

Challenges

Try these challenges for the next 30 days and then decide which ones you want to continue with for the long term.

Challenge 1 – Fail: Ask yourself at the end of the day if you failed at anything (perhaps ask the family over dinner). If you have failed, then celebrate as it means you are trying.

Challenge 2 – Create: Decide to spend at least a few minutes each day creating something. This could be a different thing each day (e.g.: a meal or a picture) or something that is created over time like writing a novel, knitting a scarf or building a treehouse.

Challenge 3 – Dream big: Think of and start to plan one or more big life goals or challenges.

Bonus 'Anytime' Challenge – Write a list of all your accomplishments, big and small from over your entire life and celebrate how great you are.

11

THE PARADOX OF AWESOMENESS

 'I'm not offended by all of the dumb blonde jokes because I know I'm not dumb ... and I also know that I'm not blonde.' – Dolly Parton

Recap

Phew! Your head may be spinning. Let's do a quick review of the main points:

- Awesomeness is your birthright—you are awesome because you are alive
- You don't have to be or do anything to prove it—you are just awesome
- Unfortunately, we lose our sense of how awesome we really are due to our learned negative thought patterns and culturally conditioned beliefs
- Our prehistoric 'lizard' brain creates a real human need

- for safety, security, certainty, control, predictability and order
- As a result of this survival mechanism we learn two primary fears: that we are not enough and so won't be loved
- The bottom line of The Lizard + Certainty + Primary Fears equation is low self-love (which can also be called low self-worth or low self-esteem)
- This lack of self-love manifests in many ways, in particular: The Four Hazards
- The Four Hazards are Perfectionism, Procrastination, People Pleasing and Playing Small (which consists of low self-esteem, imposter syndrome, nagging self-doubt or lack of self-confidence)
- The Four Hazards (P's) can be minimized or eliminated by The Four Solutions (S's) which allow you to embrace your awesomeness once more
- The Four Solutions are Self-Love, Security and Control, Social Awesomeness and Step Out of Your Comfort Zone
- Each of The Four Solutions has three Tools of Awesomeness – 12 in total:

1. Awesomeness Pep Talk
2. Self-Love Affirmations
3. Practice Self-Care
4. Rituals and Habits
5. Empowering Language
6. Tap into Your Intuition
7. Say 'No'
8. Detach from Approval and Criticism
9. Better Communication
10. Fail
11. Create
12. Dream Big

All of this will also be listed in the Appendix for easy reference.

The Paradox of Awesomeness

What is being asked of you?

- Do everything you can to feel in control AND be able to live with uncertainty
- Love yourself just as you are AND be willing to grow into your potential
- Treat yourself with kindness AND challenge yourself to be better
- Be content with your life as it is AND strive to improve and grow
- Express your opinions clearly AND shut up and listen
- Stand your ground AND be adaptable
- Be sane in an insane world

Carl Jung calls paradoxes "one of our most valued spiritual possessions." I would call them a pain in the proverbial! They are by their very nature full of uncertainty so of course it's hard to accept them. Regardless, we must trust them and navigate them in order to live life to the full and embrace our awesomeness.

What is being asked is so simple, it's just that we are constantly looking around it instead of staring straight at the bat in the cage.

You have been asked to love yourself fully. You have been asked to show your real self to the world. You have been asked to step out of your comfort zone when you can. These are all risky, vulnerable and uncertain requests. You are to go on a dark, painful journey... and for what? What can be promised in return? What is on the other side?

Deep down you know. You've felt empty for a long, long time. There is a void where you know something is missing, you have just forgotten what it is. The vague yearning feeling has been with you for as long as you can remember. You have been homesick for you.

Embracing your awesomeness means coming home.

It means coming back to your real self, your soul, your place in the universe.

Perhaps the biggest paradox of awesomeness is that what you have been longing for, what you have been homesick for has been within you all along. You wanted certainty and you wanted love and they have always been there for the taking.

Permission Slip

At the beginning of this book I gave you a permission slip. You can now tear it up. You don't need a permission slip from a book. You don't need it from me. You don't need it from anyone else. I will still be here cheering from the sidelines, but you've got this.

You ARE your own permission slip.

12

A WORLD OF AWESOMENESS

 'And now that you don't have to be perfect, you can be good.' – John Steinbeck

Quiz Time

Read the first set of questions, pause for a few seconds and then read the second set. There is no need to find out the actual answers. You won't be marked. Just read through the two quizzes and you will get the point.

First Quiz

1. Name the wealthiest person in the world
2. Name the last winner of the Miss America contest
3. Name the first person who won the Nobel Peace Prize
4. Name the director of the best picture at the Academy Awards last year

5. Name the person who got the most gold medals at the last Olympic games

Second Quiz

1. Name a teacher who helped you at school
2. Name a friend who assisted you through a tough time
3. Name three people who you enjoy spending quality time with
4. Name someone who taught you something that changed your life
5. Name one person who makes you feel loved, valued and appreciated

How did you do?

A World of Awesomeness

Imagine a world where we all embrace our innate awesomeness. What would it look like?

Sure, there would be the a few people in the first group. The ones who are the very best in the fields. The ones who are super-high achievers. The ones with the most credentials, the most money or the most awards. But in the end, we barely remember them.

What is more encouraging is the second group. This represents many unremarkable people, the ones the history books won't remember—you and me. The ones who decide to show up. The ones who love themselves enough to grow into their potential. The ones who don't let hazardous beliefs stop them from sharing their gifts. The ones who found joy, grace and beauty in the ordinary, every single day.

The ones who unreservedly embraced their awesomeness.

Become part of the second group.

Embrace your awesomeness.

Create a legacy.

Start today.

APPENDIX

Recap

- Awesomeness is your birthright—you are awesome because you are alive

- You don't have to be or do anything to prove it—you are just awesome

- Unfortunately, we lose our sense of how awesome we really are due to our learned negative thought patterns and culturally conditioned beliefs

- Our prehistoric 'lizard' brain creates a real human need for safety, security, certainty, control, predictability and order

- As a result of this survival mechanism we learn two primary fears: that we are not enough and so won't be loved

Appendix

- The bottom line of The Lizard + Certainty + Primary Fears equation is low self-love (which can also be called low self-worth or low self-esteem)

- This lack of self-love manifests in many ways, in particular: The Four Hazards

- The Four Hazards are:

  - Perfectionism
  - Procrastination
  - People Pleasing
  - Playing Small (which consists of low self-esteem, imposter syndrome, nagging self-doubt or lack of self-confidence)

- The Four Hazards (P's) can be minimized or eliminated by The Four Solutions (S's) which allow you to embrace your awesomeness once more

- The Four Solutions are:

  - Self-Love
  - Security and Control
  - Social Awesomeness
  - Step Out of Your Comfort Zone

- Each of The Four Solutions has three Tools of Awesomeness – 12 in total:

1. Awesomeness Pep Talk
2. Self-Love Affirmations
3. Practice Self-Care
4. Rituals and Habits

5. Empowering Language
6. Tap into Your Intuition
7. Say 'No'
8. Detach from Approval and Criticism
9. Better Communication
10. Fail
11. Create
12. Dream Big

Monthly Challenges

Try these challenges for the next 30 days and then decide which ones you want to continue with for the long term.

- Awesomeness pep talk: read the awesomeness pep talk to yourself once per day.

- Self-love affirmations: say self-love affirmations to yourself in the mirror for one minute per day.

- Practice self-care: make a list of your favorite self-care activities and commit to doing at least one per day.

- Rituals and habits: decide to do one positive habit every day for the next month, e.g.: go for a 20-minute walk, have a bowl of raw vegetables before dinner, say thanks at every mealtime, make your bed or spend some time reading.

- Empowering language: change at least one disempowering word or phrase to an empowering one, e.g.: remove 'should' from your vocabulary. Simply don't say those negative words. The Lizard might still think them, but don't say them out loud. I doubt anyone will notice as they are too busy rushing around being stressed. But you will feel a difference.

- Tap into your intuition: add in a daily stillness habit: pause, breathe deeply, walk in nature, meditate or sit in silence and notice your five physical senses in order to make space for you to tap into your intuition.

- Say 'no': say a polite 'no' every day—to your partner, kids, friends, work colleagues, charities, committees, sales people and anyone else who comes along. Remember 'no' is a complete sentence.

- Detach from approval and criticism: practice ignoring opinions of those who do not matter (95% of the world) and saying a simple 'thanks' to any other feedback you receive in the next month.

- Better communication: be vigilant at reworking as much of your communication as possible into warm, direct and assertive sentences, using I statements, consequences and asking for exactly what you want.

- Fail: Ask yourself at the end of the day if you failed at anything (perhaps ask the family over dinner). If you have failed, then celebrate as it means you are trying.

- Create: Decide to spend at least a few minutes each day creating something. This could be a different thing each day (e.g.: a meal or a picture) or something that is created over time like writing a novel, knitting a scarf or building a treehouse.

Appendix

- Dream big: Think of and start to plan one or more big life goals or challenges.

Bonus 'Anytime' Challenges

- Decide on your go-to extravagant compliment. Write it down and say it out loud three times whenever you are being critical of yourself.

- Adopt some practical habits you want to set up and continue with on, say, a monthly basis, e.g.: reviewing your expenses, installing a regular date night or volunteering.

- Use the phrase 'tell me more' when it is the very last thing you want to do during a tough conversation or argument.

- Write a list of all your accomplishments, big and small from over your entire life and celebrate how great you are.

If you get nothing else out of this book, then instead of asking, 'Is this true?', ask 'Is this helpful?'

READER GIFT: THE HAPPY20

Part of becoming rebelliously happy is remembering to squeeze the best out every single day. To remind you of this, I created

THE HAPPY20
20 Free Ways to Boost Happiness in 20 Seconds or Less

A PDF gift for you with quick ideas to improve mood and add a little sparkle to your day.

Head to **JulieSchooler.com/gift** and grab your copy today.

ABOUT THE AUTHOR

Julie had aspirations of being a writer since she was very young but somehow got sidetracked into the corporate world. After the birth of her first child, she rediscovered her creative side. You can find her at JulieSchooler.com.

Her *Easy Peasy* books provide simple and straightforward information on parenting topics. The *Nourish Your Soul* series shares delicious wisdom to feel calmer, happier and more fulfilled.

Busy people can avoid wasting time searching for often confusing and conflicting advice and instead spend time with the beautiful tiny humans in their lives and do what makes their hearts sing.

Julie lives with her family in a small, magnificent country at the bottom of the world where you may find her trying to bake the perfect chocolate brownie.

facebook.com/JulieSchoolerAuthor
instagram.com/julie.schooler
twitter.com/JulieSchooler

BOOKS BY JULIE SCHOOLER

***Easy Peasy* Books**

Easy Peasy Potty Training

Easy Peasy Healthy Eating

***Nourish Your Soul* Books**

Rediscover Your Sparkle

Crappy to Happy

Embrace Your Awesomeness

Bucket List Blueprint

Super Sexy Goal Setting

Find Your Purpose in 15 Minutes

Clutter-Free Forever

Children's Picture Books

Maxy-Moo Flies to the Moon

Collections

Change Your Life 3-in-1 Collection

Rebelliously Happy 3-in-1 Collection

JulieSchooler.com/books

ACKNOWLEDGMENTS

To Andrew and our two beautiful tiny humans, Dylan and Eloise. I live in a perpetual state of astonishment about how fortunate my life is. Thank you for making me laugh every single day.

PLEASE LEAVE A REVIEW

Rebelliously Happy 3-in-1 Collection

Rediscover Your Sparkle, Crappy to Happy, Embrace Your Awesomeness

THANK YOU FOR READING THIS BOOK

I devoted many months to researching and writing this book. I then spent more time having it professionally edited, working with a designer to create an awesome cover and launching it into the world.

Time, money and heart has gone into this book and I very much hope you enjoyed reading it as much as I loved creating it.

It would mean the world to me if you could spend a few minutes writing a review on Goodreads or the online store where you purchased this book.

A review can be as short or long as you like and should be helpful and honest to assist other potential buyers of the book.

Please Leave a Review

Reviews provide social proof that people like and recommend the book. More book reviews mean more book sales which means I can write more books.

Your book review helps me, as an independent author, more than you could ever know. I read every single review and when I get five-star review it absolutely makes my day.

Thanks, Julie.

BOOK REFERENCES

59 Seconds – Change Your Life in Under a Minute – Richard Wiseman (USA, 2011)

Atomic Habits – An Easy and Proven Way to Build Good Habits and Break Bad Ones – James Clear (US, 2018)

Authentic Happiness – Using the New Positive Psychology to Realize Your Potential for Lasting Fulfillment – Martin Seligman, Ph.D. (US, 2002)

Braving the Wilderness – The Quest for True Belonging and the Courage to Stand Alone – Brené Brown, Ph.D. (US, 2017)

Daring Greatly – How the Courage to be Vulnerable Transforms the Way We Live, Love, Parent and Lead – Brené Brown (US, 2013)

Do Less – A Revolutionary Approach to Time and Energy Management for Busy Moms – Kate Northrup (US, 2019)

Book References

Embracing Uncertainty: Achieving Peace of Mind as We Face the Unknown – Susan Jeffers, Ph.D. (US, 2003)

Essentialism – The Disciplined Pursuit of Less – Greg McKeown (US, 2014)

Exhausted to Energized – Dr. Libby's Guide to Living Your Life with More Energy – Dr. Libby Weaver (NZ, 2015)

Feel the Fear and Do It Anyway – How to Turn Your Fear and Indecision into Confidence and Action – Susan Jeffers (UK, 1987)

Finding Your Own North Star – How to Claim the Life You Were Meant to Live – Martha Beck (US, 2001)

Finding Your Way in a Wild New World – Reclaim Your True Nature to Create the Life You Want – Martha Beck (US, 2012)

French Children Don't Throw Food (aka *Bringing Up Bébé*) – *Parenting Secrets from Paris* - Pamela Druckerman (USA, 2013)

Girl, Stop Apologizing – A Shame-Free Plan for Embracing and Achieving Your Goals – Rachel Hollis (US, 2019)

Girl, Wash Your Face – Stop Believing the Lies About Who You Are So You Can Become Who You Were Meant to Be – Rachel Hollis (US, 2018)

Happy for No Reason – 7 Steps to Being Happy from the Inside Out – Marci Shimoff (USA, 2008)

Heal Your Soul: A Simple Guide to Understanding and Healing Yourself on a Spiritual Level to Create Greater Health, Happiness and Success – Deborah Jane Sutton (US, 2019)

Book References

How to Be an Imperfectionist – The New Way to Self-Acceptance, Fearless Living and Freedom from Perfectionism – Stephen Guise (US, 2015)

How to Win Friends and Influence People – Dale Carnegie (USA, 1953 /2006)

Love Yourself Like Your Life Depends On It – Kamal Ravikant (US, 2020)

Man's Search for Meaning – Victor E. Frankl (US, 1959 / 2006)

Minimalism – Live a Meaningful Life – Joshua Fields Millburn and Ryan Nicodemus (US, 2016)

On Being Human – A Memoir of Waking Up, Living Real and Listening Hard – Jennifer Pastiloff (US, 2019)

Playing Big – Find Your Voice, Your Vision and Make Things Happen – Tara Mohr (US, 2014)

Play It Away: A Workaholic's Cure for Anxiety – Charlie Hoehn (US, 2014)

Politically Incorrect Parenting – Before Your Kids Drive You Crazy – Nigel Latta (NZ, 2010)

Radical Acceptance – Awakening the Love that Heals Fear and Shame Within Us – Tara Brach (US, 2003)

Raising Happiness – Ten Simple Steps for More Joyful Kids and Happier Parents – Christine Carter, Ph.D. (US, 2010)

Book References

Rising Strong – The Reckoning. The Rumble. The Revolution. – Brené Brown, Ph.D. (US, 2015)

Rushing Woman's Syndrome – The Impact of a Never Ending To-Do List on your Health – Dr. Libby Weaver (NZ, 2011)

Self-Confidence – A Philosophy – Charles Pépin (UK, 2020)

Steering by Starlight – The Science and Magic of Finding Your Destiny – Martha Beck (US, 2008)

Stop Trying So F*cking Hard – Live Authentically, Design a Life You Love, and Be Happy (Finally)! – Honorée Corder (US, 2018)

The Art of Work – A Proven Path to Discovering What You Were Meant to Do - Jeff Goins (US, 2015)

The Busy Woman's Guide to High Energy Happiness – Louise Thompson (NZ, 2014)

The Choice – Embrace the Possible – Dr. Edith Eva Eger (US, 2017)

The Confidence Code – The Science and Art of Self-Assurance – What Women Should Know – Katty Kay and Claire Shipman (US, 2014)

The Dance of Anger – A Woman's Guide to Changing the Patterns of Intimate Relationships – Harriet Lerner, Ph.D. (US, 1985 / 2016)

The Dance of Intimacy – A Woman's Guide to Courageous Acts of Change in Key Relationships – Harriet Lerner, Ph.D. (US, 1990 / 1999)

The Five Love Languages – The Secret to Love that Lasts – Gary Chapman (US, 1992 / 2010)

Book References

The Gifts of Imperfection: Let Go of Who You Think You're Supposed to Be and Embrace Who You Are – Brené Brown (US, 2010)

The Happiness Project – Gretchen Rubin (USA, 2009)

The One Goal – Master the Art of Goal Setting, Win Your Inner Battles and Achieve Exceptional Results – Thibaut Meurisse (US, 2017)

The ONE Thing – The surprisingly simple truth behind extraordinary results – Gary Keller with Jay Papasan (US, 2013)

The Power is Within You – Louise Hay (US, 1991 / 2006 / 2017)

The Secret – Rhonda Byrne (US, 2006)

The Seven Habits of Highly Effective People – Restoring the Character Ethic – Steven R Covey (US, 1990)

The Subtle Art of Not Giving a F*ck – A Counterintuitive Approach to Living a Good Life – Mark Manson (US, 2016)

The Top Five Regrets of the Dying – A Life Transformed by the Dearly Departed – Bronnie Ware (US, 2011)

The Winner's Bible – Rewire Your Brain for Permanent Change – Dr Kerry Spackman (USA, 2009)

Thrive – The Third Metric to Redefining Success and Creating a Life of Wellbeing, Wisdom and Wonder – Arianna Huffington (US, 2014)

Tools of Titans: The Tactics, Routines, and Habits of Billionaires, Icons, and World-Class Performers – Tim Ferriss (US, 2016)

Book References

Visions to the Top – A Millionaire's Secret Formula to Productivity, Visualization and Meditation – Justin Ledford (US, 2016)

You are a Badass – How to Stop Doubting Your Greatness and Start Living an Awesome Life – Jen Sincero (US, 2013)

www.ingramcontent.com/pod-product-compliance
Lightning Source LLC
Chambersburg PA
CBHW051349290426
44108CB00015B/1943